LET THE
CHILDREN
COME

LET THE CHILDREN COME

Reimagining Childhood from a Christian Perspective

Bonnie J. Miller-McLemore
Foreword by Lisa Sowle Cahill

JOSSEY-BASS
A Wiley Imprint
www.josseybass.com

Published by Jossey-Bass
A Wiley Imprint
989 Market Street, San Francisco, CA 94103-1741   www.josseybass.com

Jossey-Bass books and products are available through most bookstores. To contact Jossey-Bass directly call our Customer Care Department within the U.S. at 800-956-7739, outside the U.S. at 317-572-3986 or fax 317-572-4002.

Jossey-Bass also publishes its books in a variety of electronic formats. Some content that appears in print may not be available in electronic books.

Library of Congress Cataloging-in-Publication Data
Miller-McLemore, Bonnie J.
   Let the children come: reimagining childhood from a Christian perspective / Bonnie J. Miller-McLemore; foreword by Lisa Sowle Cahill.
      p. cm.—(Families and faith series)
   Includes bibliographical references and index.
   ISBN 0-7879-5665-1 (alk. paper)
   1. Children (Christian theology)   I. Title.   II. Series.
BT705.M55 2003   2003007926
270'.083—dc21

Printed in the United States of America
FIRST EDITION
HB Printing   10 9 8 7 6 5 4 3 2 1

THE FAMILIES AND FAITH SERIES

The Families and Faith Series is devoted to exploring the relationship between the spiritual life and our closest human relationships. From one generation to the next, faith and families are deeply intertwined in powerful ways. Faith puts all of life, including family life, in such a large perspective that it invites the gratitude, wonder, and hope so badly needed in the middle of the complexities and struggles of existence. On the other hand, faith becomes real only as it lives through concrete human relationships. Religion needs families and communities where the generations gather together and share and celebrate what it means to love God and to love others. At their best, faith and families are immersed in grace, and this series hopes to be a resource for those seeking to make love real in their families, congregations, and communities.

Diana R. Garland
> Director, Baylor Center for Family and Community Ministries
> Baylor University

J. Bradley Wigger
> Director, Center for Congregations and Family Ministries
> Louisville Presbyterian Theological Seminary

SERIES EDITORS

TITLES IN THE FAMILIES AND FAITH SERIES
Sacred Stories of Ordinary Families: Living the Faith in Daily Life
> Diana R. Garland
Let the Children Come: Reimagining Childhood from a Christian Perspective
> Bonnie J. Miller-McLemore
The Power of God at Home: Nurturing our Children in Love and Grace
> J. Bradley Wigger
Seasons of a Family's Life: Cultivating the Contemplative Spirit at Home
> Wendy M. Wright
Real Kids, Real Faith: Practices for Nurturing Children's Spiritual Lives
> Karen Marie Yust

With love for my parents,
Geraldine Cobb Miller
and
John McAdow Miller

CONTENTS

———

FOREWORD

———

A wife, mother of three sons, scholar of religion and psychology, and professor of practical theology, Bonnie J. Miller-McLemore has excellent qualifications with which to address the precarious situation of children in modern North America. And she does so expertly. Her treatment is not only engagingly written and filled with common sense but also theologically illuminating and pastorally astute.

Miller-McLemore's earlier work, *Also a Mother: Work and Family as Theological Dilemma* (1994), captured the ambiguous situation of young Christian parents—especially women—who struggle to reconcile their ties and responsibilities to their families with their vocational projects and commitments in the workplace. In this new endeavor, she turns her sights from the identity and role of the parent to the identity and uniqueness of the child. While most modern theories and analyses of childhood have concentrated on adults' ideas of children, child-rearing practices, or obligations toward children, Miller-McLemore takes a hard look at the roles of children themselves in different social eras and asks what is distinctive and problematic about our own age.

She catches several confusing cultural trends that make raising children a special challenge today. For example, while we sentimentalize children and see them as immense sources of emotional satisfaction, we are afflicted with a high level of social indifference toward the welfare of other people's children. Moreover, even while pop psychology extols the "innocence" of children, they are targeted as consumers in our market-driven economy. On the one hand, parents are held morally responsible for any negative behavior on the part of children; on the other, children's desires are manipulated so that an array of products will be profitable. Society as a whole avoids providing economic support for the kinds of housing, health care, child care, and educational systems that help parents do a good job. In the face of all these stresses, strains, and outright assaults on the well-being of children, religion seems ineffectual. Churches, faith communities, and religious traditions seem to offer very few solutions or insights to the average person.

Miller-McLemore's thesis is that a religious vision can support the claim that "children must be fully respected as persons, valued as gifts, and viewed as agents." Children are not innocent "blank slates" with no God-given capacity for spiritual experience, moral awareness, or decision making. Miller-McLemore borrows the image of the "knowing child" to communicate that children often inhabit a state between nonagency and full responsibility. Sometimes they are even capable of destructive or malicious behavior. They also have a desire for God, can ask profound religious questions, and anguish when they feel responsible for wrongdoing. Miller-McLemore even recovers the category of "sin" in reference to children. While this term fell out of favor for most religious communities in the 1960s and has operated in many historical periods as an excuse for unjustifiably harsh discipline, it can be important both to identify children's legitimate responsibility and their capacity for change. Children should not be excluded from "the complex human dynamics of human failure, reconciliation, and hope." Adults have the responsibility to encourage and shape children's behavior without harshness or rigidity. Religious traditions can help us recover a sense of human frailty and grace in relation to children's moral and spiritual identity. Figures from the tradition such as Thomas Aquinas, Martin Luther, Menno Simons, John Calvin, and Jonathan Edwards can be our guides in this process.

An important implication of the position being put forward in this book is that since children are agents but are vulnerable and growing nonetheless adults have a special responsibility to make sure that they can thrive in social structures and practices that encourage virtuous behavior and nourish their awakening spiritual identities. Although all persons are formed by the institutions and practices in which they participate, children have less independent ability to resist the negative impact of distorted cultural expressions and to actively reform the world around them. Precisely because children are not innocent but knowing, parents, adults, the church, and the community in general need to deliberately reduce inducements or pressures that lead children's agency in the wrong direction. Children need to be given opportunities to take responsibility, act compassionately and responsibly for and with others, and be accountable when they have fallen short. Children need "empowerment, liberation, inclusivity, and justice." Churches can help create communities in which raising children is the responsibility and reward of all, not just of mothers or parents.

Miller-McLemore is aware of the repercussions for children of larger social injustices that take the form of sexism, racism, and class discrimination. Children can and do suffer from these distorted patterns of relationship, but children can also become involved in the struggle against evil and corruption. Children can participate in conversion and reconciliation, and they can share these experiences with others. In the Epilogue, Miller-McLemore recounts a faculty and student trip to Nicaragua, which was led by the Center for Global Education and which she holds up as the most inspirational contribution to her book project. Most U.S. citizens, she says, even the traveling do-gooders, are oblivious to the reasons our GDP is about sixty times that of Nicaragua. One of the more obvious causes is the exploitation of the poorer country's natural resources by the wealthier one. But most North Americans hope for little more for their children than their children's own happiness. During the travel seminar to Nicaragua, Miller-McLemore encountered a Christian parent named Pinita, who with her husband gave up a comfortable life to join a Catholic base community and teach her children to become involved in trying to change the lives of the poor. Miller-McLemore's concluding reflections connect her work with Christian ethics, especially the current interest in narrative and virtue ethics, as well as with literature on the family and on pastoral theology.

Ultimately, children are a gift. Though parents can try to protect them, nurture their personal growth, teach them to care for others, and remind them what it would be like to live in the kingdom of God, parents cannot determine or be accountable for their children's destiny. Though the market may exacerbate the tendency of parents to try to use children to meet their own needs and serve their own interests, this is certainly an age-old problem. Jesus' teaching and receptiveness to children overturn the idea that children are their parents' property or the idea that children should be completely subservient to adult demands. Jesus also links the character and role of a child with the meaning of discipleship—not only are disciples to become as vulnerable as children but children are capable of spiritual membership in the community of faith. Jesus is in solidarity with children. While parents can encourage children as they begin to assume the fullness of their spiritual, moral, and social vocations, parents do not finally control the outcome of the process. While being a parent is a tremendous responsibility, it is also a relationship with another person, which can be immensely rewarding and transformative. This is one important reason why Christian feminist theology advocates equal participation of men and women in the "labor of love" that is primary care for children.

Let the Children Come is a sensitive, creative, and faith-filled contribution to a burgeoning literature on marriage and families. The book illustrates brilliantly its own premise that practical theology takes ordinary experience as a fundamental resource for Christian theories about the relationship between God and humanity. It offers a powerful critique of contemporary culture while affirming the emergence of a feminist and social conscience that has only been possible with the modern age. It acclaims the worth and beauty of childhood without sentimentality or romanticization. It affirms parental responsibilities without self-righteousness or reactionary blame-casting. It mines the resources of the Christian tradition without collapsing today's demands of faith into the norms and expectations of the past. Above all, it is a freeing account of the potential for goodness and even greatness that lies hidden in the vulnerable "knowingness" of children, waiting to be drawn forth through the love of adults who accept them as gifts.

Boston, Massachusetts   Lisa Sowle Cahill
July 2003

INTRODUCTION

Faithful Parenting:
The Search for
Operating Instructions

———

When my own children were little, I hated it when parents with older offspring told me that life would not get any easier. Behind their commiseration, I heard, "You think you have it hard? Just wait." Now, with three sons eleven, thirteen, and sixteen years old, I try to refrain from making similar unfriendly observations to new parents. But sometimes I just can't help it.

In *Operating Instructions: A Journal of My Son's First Year,* Anne Lamott gives an uncannily honest, poignantly funny account of her son Sam's first year of life. She swings from moments of sheer rapture to bouts of frustration, tedium, and raw anger. She even sends notes to God in search of the next "operating instructions." We laugh as readers, for we have been there; and we sigh with relief when she ultimately finds some guidance through supportive friends and a small African American Christian congregation.

I still cannot help wondering, however, what kind of journal Lamott will write when Sam moves into his "tweens," the term the business world has concocted for consumers ages eight to fourteen. What will faithful parenting look like when you have to fight with the market, other parents, and other cultural pressures over your child's desires, ambitions, and ultimate commitments? How will communications with God and the Christian community figure in?

As those parents of older children predicted, the demands do not ease up. They simply change and, in most cases, become more difficult to manage. The increased difficulties are partly a natural consequence of dealing with older children and youth. But problems today also have a lot to do with radical reconstruction of childhood and heightened demands on children and parents.

With small children, struggles revolve around the daily trial-and-error, hit-and-miss process of figuring out their basic needs. Even though this effort intensifies life, it takes place primarily within the home. Mothers of young children—and, increasingly, some fathers—struggle with vocational questions about juggling family and paid employment or balancing the needs of self and child, often torn between powerful religious assumptions about parental sacrifice and equally persuasive psychological presumptions about pursuing self-fulfillment. As children grow, however, the problem is not so much feeling torn or making a choice between two vocations as being torn by multiple demands and living with the actual choices made. The struggle stretches far beyond the confines of the home, to the wider social arena in which children and parents are bombarded by multiple and sometimes staggering expectations.

If nursing an infant is, as Lamott remarks, "the easiest, purest communication I've ever known," then daily communication with intimate family members over the long haul is among the hardest. With older children, one has a larger world with which to contend. This world enters one's life sometimes wholly unbidden, just as sugar-filled cereals, Nintendo 64, a trampoline, and paintball guns entered ours, through our children's many (sometimes seemingly relentless) desires and requests. Perhaps this is why Lamott and other women have written powerful accounts of early motherhood but seldom delve into the experiences of long-term parenting. After the first few years, the waters become incredibly muddy.

From whom do parents seek guidance when the challenge becomes more complex and wide ranging than how to make it through the day with an infant without losing one's mind? What does faithful parenting, from infancy until primary responsibility shifts to the adult-child, look like today?

One cannot answer this question, I have come to realize, without grappling with important prior questions. What are the dominant cultural perceptions of children, including religious perceptions, with which parents must deal? Are there better alternatives? How should people rightfully view children in a time of great transition and turmoil?

When I began to write about the dilemmas of early parenting after my first son was born, I tried to be as candid as Lamott about the surprising trials and tribulations, especially about how the very commitment to mothering could both impede and sustain my energies for such reflection. I also attempted to be honest about the value and the limits of Christianity's governing perceptions of children and good parenting. As much as I hated to hear it, however, a few readers suggested new questions would arise with older children. They certainly have.

I genuinely did not expect, I honestly admit, that each of my children would become such an intricate constellation of relationships, needs, demands, problems, and gifts. Nor did I anticipate the development of an acute empathy for children as a silenced and overlooked group in society and in contemporary Christianity in particular. Ultimately, I did not realize how overwhelmed and ill equipped I would feel in becoming a parent in today's world, nor how frustrated I would become about personal and social irresponsibility toward children in general. No wonder I found myself laughing with recognition when Lamott admits she thought having a child would resemble getting a cat! How is it that most of us have so misperceived the realities of child bearing and rearing?

My children's needs and desires cause me to question many prominent cultural values. In more Christian language, they call me to account as they reveal ways in which my family and the Christian community fall short of Christian ideals about children and the good life. Most centrally, I have found myself constantly challenged to keep at bay powerful cultural trends and to probe the nature of my faith commitments as I express them to my children. I am especially troubled by the middle-class obsession with securing success for one's own children with hardly a thought for other children; and, paired with this, the extent to which parents use their children's accomplishments in soccer or math or violin to somehow feel better about themselves. From where did such an overriding perception of children evolve? How does one grapple with this as a Christian parent? What are, I ask, some of the primary revolutions in views of children? Do Christianity's most basic convictions have anything to say about them? These core questions form the bedrock of this book.

In my search for answers, I turn to sources that many people would not think to put into the same conversation: Christianity, feminism, and psychology. I am convinced, however, that much is gained from drawing these parties into richer dialogue. As a Christian feminist mother and a scholar of religion and psychology, my research naturally emerged out of my own personal frustrations with the limitations of Christian, psychological, and feminist views, and at the same time my belief that all three have important insights to offer.

Many people today seldom see Christianity as a credible or relevant resource. Mainstream congregations have not seemed too interested in current child-rearing dilemmas. Meanwhile, contemporary theologians mostly neglect the subject. "Real" theology in the last century focused on adults. After Horace Bushnell, well known for his mid-nineteenth-century theology of childhood, the door slammed shut on children as a respectable topic. Theologians who have recently reconsidered families as part of the marriage movement comment on children's plight, but often as a means to another end—that of revitalizing marriage.

Meanwhile, contemporary psychology is probably the number one authority on children. But it is frequently accused of promoting only selfish pursuit of individual adult fulfillment. Thanks to psychology's portrayal of abusive Christian ideas, people know a lot more about the damage Christianity has done than they do about its value.

About the only place Christian views of child rearing receive extraordinary attention is from the huge conservative conglomerate Focus on the Family, which stubbornly resists the revolutionary changes in the last century in women and children's roles. Yet feminists who have welcomed greater equality for women do not fare much better than mainstream Christianity when it comes to child-rearing advice. It has been hard for feminists, both secular and religious, to avoid the pitfall of pitting women's needs and children's needs against one another. Many men in the field of religion do not regard children as a credible subject of study because of their *distance* from domestic care, but most women have not taken up the topic because of their *proximity* to children and to the sometimes-onerous immersion in their daily care.

Finally, a pluralistic, diverse postmodern society makes the particularities of Christianity itself suspect. Books sell when they put "spiritual" in the title. But put "Christian" there, and you doom the publication to a limited readership.

Still, even though the resources of Christianity, feminism, and psychology do not cohabit the same space well, some real benefits come from sparking conversation. A major reinvention of childhood is under way. Christianity—as found in its early traditions, corrected by contemporary psychological insights, and revised by recent feminist understandings—must be a ready participant in figuring out who children are and why we should care about them.

What does it look like to reconsider children with integrity and faithfulness as a feminist Christian in a complex postmodern society? My hope is that fresh visions of childhood will emerge. Themes central to psychology, Christianity, and feminism confirm my main thesis: children must be fully respected as persons, valued as gifts, and viewed as agents. Although advertisements and political pundits also spout these same three premises, and they seem like commonplace knowledge, their Christian roots and their riveting implications have been consistently and sorely trivialized and underestimated. Women and men of faith will best supply what children need when these ideals are more boldly proclaimed. This will happen only when religious communities help by upholding these visions, and when care for children is viewed as a practice of the entire community, not simply of parents or mothers alone. Child rearing and responsibility for how children are viewed belongs to all Christians. This contests the modernist privatization and truncation of both religion and children, and it calls for the greater public role of a reinterpreted Christianity in reimagining children.

Christianity continues to shape how we think about children more than most of us realize. Attempting a cultural overhaul in the value and vision of children will not get far without more careful attention to it. Many social scientists, public intellectuals, and popular writers, for example, want to challenge our poisonous popular culture and the public morality of materialism, big business, and commercialization of children without grasping the critical role that religion—specifically, Christian theology—might play. To effect genuine cultural change requires careful exploration, critique, and revision of religion as a key culture-forming institution.

Religious faith is not a purely personal, nonrational conviction; it shapes both our history and our normative visions. It involves a historically developed body of traditions and practices that shape communities, rituals, and lives. It provides moral and spiritual language and frameworks of meaning that help us make sense of the ups and downs of family life and that help us question human distortions and perversions. Even in a postmodern context where cultural diversity renders universal truths impossible, people still need and search for ideals and frameworks by which to live. Politicians and parents alike would benefit from richer understanding of traditions that have considered children in specifically religious and moral terms. Various religious traditions, including Christianity, have long seen children as an invaluable part of the common good and hence a public concern. In some ways, reclaiming religion's importance in the public square involves reclaiming children's public value.

It is important to clarify that this is not a book about *how children think in general* or about *how children think about God*. Nor is it a book on *how to raise children in Christian faith*. When I first received a grant for this research and news reached the general public, this was the general assumption of newspersons, my neighbors, and my kids' teachers. Perhaps this was an easier or simpler way to understand the book than what I had in mind. These are indeed important subjects, and the book's reflections certainly have implications for these other three tasks. It even took me a while to become clear, however, that this is a book about *how adults think about children* (a descriptive task) and about *how adults should think about children* (a prescriptive or normative task).

I began this book believing I was writing about raising children from a Christian perspective. But I soon discovered that I could not write a child-rearing book until I contested dominant cultural views of children and figured out better ways to think about them.

We assume we know all about children. But the ground under foot is constantly shifting. Assumed visions inherited from bygone Christianity and modern science no longer fit, yet new controlling images suggested by politics, popular psychology, and the market are inadequate and sometimes outright destructive. This book, then, is about that convulsing ground on which children and caring adults stand: the images that are failing us; the battle over new ways to understand children; the distortions toward which many people, including myself, are tempted; and the attempt to assert healthier, richer moral and religious visions. Reimagining children, I am convinced, will lead to a renewed conception of the care of children as a religious practice.

AUTHOR'S NOTE

A Practical Theology
of Children

———

This book is for the thoughtful lay reader—whether a parent, person of faith, or social scientist with an interest in children and religion—and not just for the academic theologian. Nonetheless, I want to explain briefly the book's place in the study of theology for two reasons. First, lay readers deserve to know something about how the study of theology is organized. Second, academic theologians ought to know more about new developments in the area of practical theology in which this book falls.

Many people do not understand the study of Christianity in colleges, universities, seminaries, and divinity schools because those who study theology have not done a good job communicating what theologians do. How does one study Christianity, and how is this related to or different from believing in it? How can people talk about Christianity without getting mired down by confessional faith claims that, in their personal and nonrational nature, do not seem to have any public relevance? Not only should systematic, historical, and biblical theologians pay greater heed to this educative task, they ought to know what is happening in the area of practical theology. This book is basically an effort in practical theology.

Making children a central theological concern challenges the generally accepted categories of study in theology—what has been called the "theological encyclopedia." This term refers to the nineteenth-century organization of the study of religion into the four self-defined areas of biblical, historical, systematic, and practical reflection. This schema goes back to Friedrich Schleiermacher's efforts to secure a home for religion in the modern European university in the nineteenth century. Many theologians who inherited this framework assigned practical theology a fairly circumscribed role. It concerned professional acts of congregational ministry as performed by either clergy or laity. As such, it was primarily the application of theoretical truths discovered in biblical, historical, and doctrinal theology to concrete church situations. Even today, many theologians bracket practical theology as peripheral to the more important theoretical work of biblical, historical, and constructive theology. Even the way in which theological schools are organized as institutions makes it hard not to misperceive systematic, historical, and biblical theology as the "real work" of theology, and practical theology as simply the application of this work to acts of ministry. Studying children, however, necessarily challenges these traditional categories.

Choosing the subject matter of children, I believe, requires a radical rethinking of the theological encyclopedia, including a fundamental redefinition of practical theology itself. To think about children theologically requires movement across the conventionally separated disciplines. This movement includes moments of serious historical, biblical, and constructive theological exploration as part of a larger practical theological effort. One must know about contemporary dilemmas as they arise out of a particular Christian history, as related to specific biblical texts and doctrinal themes, and in response to new possibilities for children in today's world. That is, studying children requires movement from an exploration of dilemmas (Chapter One and the first part of Chapter Two) to an investigation of Christian resources (the second part of Chapter Two and Chapters Three through Six) back to a renewed practice (Epilogue).

A practical theology of children has the role of mediating between powerful religious symbol systems and the wider society. It tries to bridge the gap that sometimes arises between the efforts of systematic theologians to shape a Christian worldview and the daily practices that actually form such a world. As a rule, systematic theologians are better at shaping overarching worldviews and formal doctrines than at monitoring how people practice their faith and actually live out these ideas on a daily basis. A practical theology of childhood takes this additional

Author's Note

step. In dealing with religious texts, the final aim is different from systematic, biblical, and historical theology. The aim is to understand what is going on in order to effect change in a situation and in the theological ideas that define it.

Childhood is not a purely theoretical concern, although children can certainly be studied in theory. Raising children is at heart a practice that engages a rich variety of developed and undeveloped theories. Practical theological knowledge about children therefore involves investigation of the "wisdom of experience," or of the thought that has developed from the practices of being raised and in turn raising children. Reimagining childhood takes us into the difficult-to-chart territory of accrued Christian wisdom and the challenge of assessing its place in today's practices. To study children theologically therefore demands study of the conceptual schemes and vocabulary that develop within the practices surrounding children, and those that have arisen in history and culture.

Making childhood the main focus raises a few methodological and moral questions. How can adults genuinely understand children? How can we appreciate the diversity of childhood and its social and political construction across cultures and history? These questions are actually sparked by a hearty feminist commitment to respect for the voice and experience of the subject. Women have contended for many years with claims about universal human experience that disregarded their views. Children likewise must be seen as actors in their own right. Claims for children's subjectivity, however, cannot come at the cost of women's relatively new-fashioned recognition as subjects.

One way to proceed is to consider children from the perspective of "feminist maternal theology." As I define it in *Also a Mother,* a feminist maternal theology draws upon knowledge located within the practices of mothering as one means to better understand children and other subjects. In this book, then, I ask not only how fresh understandings of children might influence motherhood but also how contemporary experiences of mothering shape understandings of children. Many feminist theologians have not only thought about children; they have acted as primary caregivers. Women may be enabled to hear children precisely because they have stood where children have stood, at the intersection of society's contradictory outward idealization and subtle devaluation of child care and children.

It is precisely from this vantage point that feminist theologians have distinctive contributions to make. Maternal thinking has already shaped pivotal insights in feminist theology. When Valerie Saiving first put forth the idea—revolutionary for its time—that sin in women does not lie in prideful self-assertion (as many men had defined it) but in self-loss and self-denigration, she drew heavily upon her own experience as a single mother raising a young daughter while doing graduate study in the late 1950s. Equally provocative challenges to other Christian ideas, such as conceptions of sexuality, Christ's sacrificial atonement, love as self-sacrifice, and Christian vocation, have evolved as a result of maternal thinking.

Feminist maternal theology extends four core premises in new directions. First, the demand to give privileged voice to the marginalized is extended to mothers and children. Second, feminist maternal theology challenges the contradictory demonization and idealization of children and women's bodies in the acts of bearing and raising children. Third, it enriches debate about theological doctrines of Christian love, sin, and grace by turning to the complex questions of love between the unequal parties of adult and child. Finally, a feminist maternal theology stretches claims for justice and liberation across differences to include children and mothers for whom the democratic principle of equality based on formal identity or sameness with the adult male simply does not work.

Broadly speaking, the practical feminist theological method of this book promotes two important agendas: reflection on daily life as central to theology, and respect for the voices of the marginalized as a guiding norm. Reflection on children embodies the theological conviction that the divine manifests itself in the mundane and that genuine liberation must occur in the most common of places: in the embodied lives of children. A bolder Christian vision of children is needed not only for children's sake but also for the sake of public discussion, and for the sake of an academic theology that in its erudite deliberations has lost touch with the lively unpredictability of life with children.

Author's Note

LET THE CHILDREN COME

Chapter 1

DEPRAVED, INNOCENT, OR KNOWING

History Reinvents Childhood

———

The longing for "operating instructions" (to recall Anne Lamott's phrase from the discussion in my Introduction) for child rearing did not emerge out of thin air. Today's intense anxiety about how to bring up children is the direct outcome of a series of "domestic revolutions," as historians Steven Mintz and Susan Kellogg call the far-reaching transformations in American family life of the last three centuries. These changes have raised what might be called the Child Question: What will become of children in a greatly changed world in which they no longer seem to fit easily or well? This chapter traces the twists and turns that led to modernity's fundamentally unsatisfying answer: the redefinition of children as economically useless, emotionally priceless, so-

1

cially invisible, and in the end morally and spiritually innocent.

ECONOMIC SHIFTS: CHILDREN AS ASSET OR BURDEN?

———

A few years ago, on an elementary school field trip to a 4-H agricultural center, I listened as a woman explained the processes of dairy production on a farm in bygone years to two classrooms of third-grade children. She displayed an antique butter churn and several other implements used to get butter from cow to table. Who, she asked, did they think churned the butter? Blank stares led her to hint, "Do you have chores?" "No" was the resounding chorus of about fifty eight-to-nine-year-olds. In the distribution of farm labor—not all that long ago—children close to their age churned the butter. That children no longer see themselves as directly responsible for family welfare may seem like a small matter. But in actuality it exemplifies a sea change of great proportions.

In a well-known and widely debated theory about childhood, historian Philip Ariès sees the "idea of childhood" as a "discovery" of the seventeenth century. Until that time, childhood was not considered a distinct developmental stage. Children were perceived largely as tiny adults, or at least as adults in the making. Scholars of all sorts have contested this claim, demonstrating a real appreciation for childhood prior to the modern period. Perhaps a poor English translation of Ariès's

LET THE CHILDREN COME

French term *sentiment* as simply *idea* has contributed to the confusion. By *sentiment,* he did not necessarily mean that childhood itself did not exist; rather, childhood did not carry the emotional freight that it has acquired since that time.

The debate over historical accuracy aside, however, Ariès was right on at least two accounts. Each historical period fashions its own unique attitude toward children. Equally important, a profound change occurred with the advent of modernity, which raised new questions about a child's place in society that have plagued parents up to the present day. What is it, then, about the Enlightenment, the Industrial Revolution, and today's continued technological and social innovations that has displaced children and raised distinct difficulties for families?

Although in premodern and early modern times children remained subordinates in a highly structured, patriarchal family, they had essential roles. As soon as they were old enough, they took their place in family industries, weeding and hoeing gardens, herding domestic animals, carding and spinning wool, making clothing, and caring for younger brothers and sisters. The seventeenth-century American family in general existed as a more cohesive whole, bringing together under one roof the labors of economic production, domestic life, social interaction, and political participation. As family historian John Demos puts it, "All could feel—could *see*—the contributions of the others; and all could feel the underlying framework of reciprocity." Children may have had to subordinate their interests to family and community needs and submit to the arbitrary authority of harsh fathers or weary mothers, but they knew where they stood in relationship to the family's well-being.

With industrialization, children, like women, gradually lost their place as contributing members of household economies. This shift occurred more slowly for girls and for working-class and slave children, whose labor in textile mills and coal mines or as field and domestic workers initially made it possible for white middle-class mothers and children to retreat to a private realm. Eventually, however, with emancipation, mandatory education, and child labor laws in the last century, the end result was much the same for almost all U.S. children. No longer participants in home industries, or farmed out as servants and apprentices and eventually banned from factories, children did not increase a family's chances of survival but instead drained limited resources. Their position in the family changed dramatically from asset to burden.

I do not question here the real value of protecting children from adult work. Horrendous reports of children's exploitation internationally reinforce the positive advances behind child labor laws and other changes. I am troubled, however, by a disturbing underside of a revolution in children's economic role. One of my son's working definitions of adulthood and childhood is based on his idea that "you work, I don't." Referring to some dislikable household chore, he explained, "You're the adult. You're supposed to do that; I'm not." Researchers fall into the same trap. Time-use studies of housework almost always focus on what adults do. Children drop out of the picture entirely.

Parents have struggled with how to fit children back in. Resistance to the idea of children as workers has led to the wrongheaded assumption that sharing domestic labor goes inherently against the grain of genuine childhood. Although a family allowance offers a solution to children's exclusion from the cash economy, even here common child-rearing advice argues against letting it function as a direct payment for house chores. That comes too close to giving a child an earned wage. When most U.S. parents assign chores, therefore, they do so for strikingly different reasons than in preindustrial times or in developing countries. Household tasks are considered "good" for children because they cultivate valuable character traits of altruism and reliability or teach skills that will be needed when children "grow up." They are something supposedly done out of love or duty, and not because families need children's material or financial contributions. Sometimes, when parents weigh the poorer job, the extra time, and the nagging needed to get "help," they simply resort to doing the job themselves.

Ultimately, commodification of children has become increasingly harder to resist. Estimates of the expense of raising a child make regular headline news. In 1980, not that long before my oldest son was born in 1986, it was reported that children would cost parents between $100,000 and $140,000. One June day more recently, when I presented this overview at an academic meeting, a colleague, in response to my remarks, pulled out an editorial cartoon from the daily news showing two parents holding a newspaper with the headline "Cost of Children

History Reinvents Childhood

$233,530." Turning to look at their slouching teenager with headphones and baseball cap on backwards, they remark, "Seems our investment's taken a downturn." This public pricing of children as a major family liability, something foreign less than a century ago, epitomizes the revolution that has occurred in daily life.

PSYCHOLOGICAL COMPENSATION: CHILDREN AS PRICELESS

This sweeping historical change, however, does not necessarily mean that children are any less cherished. To the contrary. What would become of children now? From the nineteenth century until today, children became even more precious in a new way. Ironically, the more productively useless children became and the less valuable in the "real" world, the more emotionally priceless they became within the home.

With the benefits of children less obvious, their desirability and even presence in the family seemed to require fresh explanation. Almost as if overcompensating for expelling children from the adult world, debate has raged in the years since industrialization about the amount of attention adults should lavish on them. Early on, new social science experts on the intricacies of child rearing, aided by Christian theologians commenting on the true nature of sacrificial love, happily offered variations on an answer. Children are to be inordinately and unconditionally loved in the private sphere of home and family—that is, loved without limit on parental excess or expectation of return on the child's part.

Every bit as captivating and virulent as the "cult of womanhood" in the nineteenth century, which extolled the piety, purity, and passivity of wives and mothers, was the "cult of childhood" and the obsession with child rearing. The very idea that improper maternal love could permanently harm a child's development, dictating how they would turn out as adults, was virtually unheard of in the Middle Ages. But by early modernity, children were idealized as precious, delicate, and in need of vigilant and constant care.

Over time, this perceived dependency became more acute in its length and nature. Puritan childhood in the 1600s was relatively brief, ending around the age of seven, followed by an extended period of transitional dependency during which young people assumed a variety of responsibilities. Contemporary childhood has doubled or even tripled, from seven to fourteen to twenty-one years. At the same time, the age of puberty has dropped, creating an odd period of physical maturity in the midst of emotional and social dependence. The number of children per family also declined, leaving parents focused upon fewer and fewer children.

Contemporary sociologists have mistaken the appropriation of the family's social, economic, and educational functions by schools, hospitals, banks, government agencies, and charitable organizations with the idea that the family is doing less. Nothing could be further from the truth. To the job of meeting a child's material needs was added the illusive, ever-expanding task of managing emotional and social development, including the very creation of meaning and fulfillment that society now falters in providing. Many parents today experience a sharp escalation of role expectations beyond anything imagined by their own parents, managing countless family interactions with multiple publics and with less and less control over those institutions that shape children.

The image of childhood as a sanctioned time and space, however, has had a distinct middle-class European American flavor that coincides with covert disinterest in the often-dire situation of other less-favored children. Less-privileged classes and nationalities, especially children in underdeveloped countries, have not lived by this modern construction of childhood and at times indirectly suffer the consequences of those who try to uphold it. It might even be argued that the protected, safe, and unproductive play of U.S. middle-class children has been largely subsidized by the labor of the working classes and less-privileged children both in the United States and around the world.

SOCIAL INVISIBILITY: CHILDREN SEEN BUT NOT HEARD

That some children were prized and child rearing made sacred did not mean that children as a whole assumed center stage. Throughout these domestic revolutions of the last several generations, children moved farther and farther from the center of adult activity and more and more into a separate, privatized realm of home, school, and church. Children lost steady contact not just with parents but with the wider world of nonfamily adults. If there is anything to be envied about children who live close to poverty, it is precisely their often-greater proximity to adults caught in the same situation.

The growing invisibility of children had a lot to do with the heightened division between private and public worlds. Fathers, increasingly removed from home to factory, shop, or office, gradually traded roles, from primary parent in child rearing and custody disputes in the seventeenth century to the often-distant provider of the late nineteenth and twentieth centuries. Children gradually spent a greater portion of time in age-segregated institutions, whether school or Sunday school. They experienced even less adult interaction in the last half century as women followed men into the workplace and daytime activity in neighborhoods diminished. In recent years, these changes have led to artificial means of bringing children and adults together, such as "take a daughter to work" or "take a grandparent to school" days, or in Christian contexts "children's sermons" and "youth Sundays."

With the rise of the middle-class companionate family in early-twentieth-century United States, the family's purpose itself became increasingly defined around personal desires. Its primary focus shifted progressively from the parent-child relationship to the couple. Marriage and family were expected to bring love, emotional connection, and fulfillment rather than property, security, and sustenance. These redefined goals did not fit all that well with one of the results of such intimacy: children. Long before the feminism of the midtwentieth century, therefore, parenting and children began to lose their ascribed status in the larger scheme of adult life.

Children were to "be seen but not heard." This English proverb first appeared in the nineteenth century, according to one dictionary of quotations, even though it was used as early as the 1400s with reference to maids rather than children. Its familiar ring today speaks volumes about the marginalization of "inferiors": women and servants initially, and then children. In the adult business of modernity, adults gazed upon children with adoration, but children had better keep quiet.

Even the artifacts used by and for children reveal this need for control and containment. In a fascinating study of changes in the material culture surrounding child rearing, historian Karin Calvert observes that "most children's furniture of the seventeenth century was designed to stand babies up and propel them forward" into adulthood and away from the precariousness of early childhood. In contrast, by the middle of the nineteenth century, cribs, high chairs, and perambulators replaced the objects designed to assimilate children rapidly into adult society. These new inventions served instead as barriers, carefully preserving a child's special sphere and designed to "hold infants down and contain them in one spot."

Today children are often expected to fit in with adult lives and choices. Adults often overprogram children, push them ahead in school, require them to use daily planners to organize their schedules, and essentially force them to grow up quickly. The multiple drop-off lanes meant for use by cars and the lack of bike racks at the school to which we moved when our children were all in elementary school epitomize the disinclination to appreciate children's views. Only adult drivers can reach the school. One cannot approach it with a child's sole means of transportation—on foot or bike. That youths get into the most trouble in the hours between 3:00 and 5:00 P.M. also speaks tellingly of the incongruity between adult and child worlds. The daily 8:00 A.M. to 3:00 P.M. schedule and the rest of the school calendar have only a distant correspondence with the daily work hours and annual holidays of the adult work world.

Even demographically, children have come to occupy an ever-shrinking place in adult lives. In the nineteenth century, only about 20 percent of families did not include children younger than eighteen. By 1991, at least 42 percent of all families did not include children. The most common living arrangement in the United States in 1998 was unmarried people without children, doubling in just a few decades from 16 percent of all families in 1972 to 32 percent. In the twenty-first century, as more young people choose to postpone marriage or remain single and childless, and as those who bear children live longer after their children leave home, a majority of households will not include children.

This is not just a matter of numbers. It is also a matter of money and its distribution. Among households without children, the median income per person is 67 percent higher than among those with two children. Some economists have responded to this statistic by suggesting policies to redistribute income from households without children to those with them. That such a reallotment is hardly imaginable in U.S. society, unless forced by governmental tax allowances or credits, underscores the extent to which most U.S. citizens do not believe they share responsibility for anyone else's children. This distinctively Western European view stands out when compared with some African governments that purposely tax the childless precisely because it is believed that all adults, especially those without children, have a financial and moral responsibility for members of the extended family.

It is the state of poor children, however, that most epitomizes the problem of the displacement of children from public view. The private sentimentalization of children and child rearing, it seems, has been inversely related to a collective indifference toward other people's children. The contradictions are grim. The heightened pace of middle-class children's extracurricular activities and the billions of dollars in available discretionary income, so sought by market specialists, contrasts sharply with the lack of opportunities and resources for the large number U.S. children living in poverty. Some parents invest in private schools and educational funds while others buy burial coverage for their child's premature death. As the U.S. economy grew by approximately 20 percent in the 1980s, four million more children moved into poverty, making up the largest proportion of poor persons in the nation. As Daniel Patrick Moynihan remarks, "There is no equivalent in our history for such a number or such a proportion."

MORAL AND RELIGIOUS QUANDARIES: DEPRAVED OR INNOCENT?

———

Hand in hand with the view of the child as productively useless but emotionally priceless and yet increasingly invisible are the redefinition of children as morally and spiritually innocent and the erasure of childhood as a vital moral and religious phase of development. Before the eighteenth century, parents may have treated the care of children casually, but attention to children's moral and religious development was anything but casual. On this score, premodern adults took children very seriously. Children entered the world bearing the marks of "original sin," an affliction associated with pride, self, and above all will. A primary parental task was to suppress and control what was seen as a child's natural depravity. Hence, some religious advice literature urged the head of household to "break" and "beat down" the will through weekly catechism, daily prayer and scripture reading, repeated admonitions, and sometimes intense psychological and even physical reprimand.

By the end of the eighteenth century, fewer people accepted this portrayal. The child's mind is a blank slate, philosopher John Locke argued, upon which anything may be imprinted. The child is by nature social and affectionate, not sinful, Jean-Jacques Rousseau said. By the midnineteenth century, the emphasis had almost entirely shifted, although certainly not within all religious circles. Children were defined as morally neutral, even "innocent" and "sacralized."

One of the most powerful illustrations of this shift appears in the evolution of children's portraits. In colonial representations, children of the upper class wear grown-up fashions and adopt a regal stance, with hands on hips and one leg extended, designed to indicate their future adult status. By the mideighteenth century, such personification of adultlike children was replaced by the endearing, soft image of the naturally innocent child. Children were endowed with an almost celestial goodness, pure and unsullied by worldly corruption.

This change marks a major shift in understanding of moral agency and accountability. In the premodern view of *imperfect children in a fallen world,* responsibility for human evil and failure was more evenly distributed among children, parents, community, government, and church. With the rise of *perfectible children in an imperfect world,* blame for problems increasingly moved away from the child. Views of children as innocent robbed them of agency.

Previously, parents located life's major threat in childhood with its dangers of disease, sin, and death. In the nineteenth century, the danger moved to adulthood and society with its threat of worldly contamination. Parents were obliged to protect children from social threats, of which there seemed to be increasingly more. In particular, as God's sovereignty and children's moral duties shrank, maternal obligations expanded. Emotional nurture became more important than moral and religious discipline. If children demonstrated selfishness or aggression, it was assumed that they were being improperly cared for, rather than something inherent to their moral or spiritual nature. This pattern of seeing faulty child rearing as the source of delinquency, poverty, violence, and other major social problems continues today.

The most prominent theologian to address child rearing in the nineteenth century, Horace Bushnell, kindly offered religious justification for this shift. His book *Christian Nurture* deified the household and Christianized emotional care. A child was still born spiritually and morally disabled, but a faithful family environment offered a handy remedy. In fact, every act of parental tenderness, every word and deed, mattered. Devotion to one's own children could itself be justified as salvific.

If child-rearing problems were no longer related so much to sin as to emotional needs, however, who cared any longer what theologians had to say? Gradually parents looked less and less to the church and more and more to secular experts. In the fuss over the "child question" of what would become of children, social scientists more than church leaders and theologians began to provide the answers. Child psychology especially mushroomed after World War II. Child care became a prominent subject of laboratory study in major universities, academic journals devoted to child development multiplied, and the population of child experts grew to include not only pediatricians, psychologists, psychiatrists, and educators but sociologists and anthropologists as well. Increasingly, religious leaders looked to social science to offer a framework for thinking about childhood, not simply by choice but by necessity. Culture afforded science much higher prestige than religion, especially when it came to understanding children.

An explosion in popular books matched the growth in academic literature. Child care manuals became the new bible for proper motherhood, epitomized initially by Dr. Spock's best-selling 1968 edition of *Baby and Child Care,* released again after 179 previous paperback printings of the original 1945 edition. Like the scientific engineering behind home economics and interior design, child rearing became a job that could be methodically mastered and children became a product to be managed and perfected.

Under the reign of children as innocent, many mainstream Christians gradually lost language with which to think of children as moral and spiritual beings. They also lost habits and practices that explicitly made space for religion on a daily basis. In particular, in the increasingly secular environment surrounding the last four generations, intentional routine family religious practices—Bible reading, prayer, discussion of faith and values, and other shared religious disciplines—lapsed. Fewer people saw the family as a valuable site for spiritual formation or knew how to make it so.

Yet without religious vocabulary and practices, people cannot talk theologically about children or implement these basic beliefs in child rearing. Fuzzy God language; distant knowledge of scripture; and the slow demise of intentional, routine household religious practices all made it harder to establish beliefs and practices that stand up well to competing views of children. In fact, when I talked with parents about parenting and faith in individual conversation and in a series of focus groups in several congregations, the one question that consistently stumped my audience was "What do your religious and moral beliefs have to do with how you raise your children?" People could name the problems of culture or of "managing our children's lives and time," but it was almost as if they had lost language with which to describe their most fundamental commitments about children.

In the past half-century, modern science and its growing public became fascinated with a peculiarly modern question: Why do children turn out the way they do? Scientific answers to this question, debating nature and nurture, largely replaced moral and religious deliberation about innocence and depravity. In fact, Judith Harris, author of the much-discussed *The Nurture Assumption,* actually declares nature and nurture, or what psychology used to call heredity and environment, the "yin and yang, the Adam and Eve, the Mom and Pop of pop psychology." Many parents in turn became more and more obsessed with doing the right thing. Science led them to believe that children and parents are perfectible, infinitely open to human design, rather than flawed and imperfect. Like a silent spiritual contagion, this preoccupation with lavishing the very best on one's own children and the inevitability of failure has spread from mothers to fathers, single parents, stepparents, grandparents, and even siblings.

No wonder recent books challenging myths about how early parenting alters brain development, for example, sell so many copies. People are eager to be relieved of guilt. Harris herself concludes that psychology has tricked us: peers matter, children socialize other children, but parents are not responsible. A chapter on "What Parents Can Do" ends with an especially gratifying section titled "The Guilt Trip Stops Here"; it reads like a recipe to ease our heavy load. Does this, however, offer a satisfactory answer to the deeper moral and spiritual questions that still lurk behind these new views of childhood?

KNOWING CHILDREN: MORAL AND RELIGIOUS QUESTIONS RETURN

We now stand in the midst of a major reconstruction in our understandings of children comparable to what occurred with the romanticization of the child in the eighteenth century, a portrayal of childhood that has now run its course. Just as the new construction of innocent childhood caused anxiety and resistance in its time, so also does the reinvention of childhood today.

A multitude of negative images already encountered in our discussion vie for position in redefining childhood: the hurried child forced to keep up with adult schedules and ideals; the market child made into an investment, consumer, and ultimately a burden; and the neglected or endangered child threatened by selfish parents or hostile social and economic structures. The general consensus behind all of these prominent constructions is that children are worse off, at least by comparison with the innocent, romanticized child that each of these depictions leaves behind.

Why are these facts and the images behind them—the hurried child, the market child, and the neglected or endangered child—so deeply disturbing? These images are desperate cultural attempts to figure out where and how children will now fit in. These views are particularly distressing because they upset cherished nineteenth-century conventions of idyllic childhood, revealing the artificiality and limitations of the invention of childhood innocence. Moreover, they contest the sharp line drawn between adult and child worlds. They show the inevitable and sometimes severe consequences for children of adult actions in the so-called separate adult realm. They insist that adults once again take children's lives more seriously, including their moral and religious struggles. Together, these images point toward a more apt characterization of postmodern children. We have moved irrevocably beyond the sentimental toward some other vision, what art historian Anne Higonnet identifies as "Knowing children."

Higonnet's characterization of the new emerging vision is apt and helpful. In place of the ideal of innocence, knowing children call into question children's "psychic and sexual innocence by attributing to them consciously active minds and bodies." The ideology of innocence meant that adults saw children as cute but less often as capable, intelligent, desiring individuals in their own right. Innocence allowed adults to picture children as passive, trivial, and available to adult objectification, exploitation, and abuse. Absolute distinctions between adult and child especially stranded adolescents, as if they ought to metamorphose overnight from one to the other and spare adults the real complexity of human life. It is difficult to tolerate the ambiguity that teenagers represent in a world still partly defined by nineteenth-century ideals.

More than anything, however, the more realistic, less romanticized knowing child mixes together sexual, moral, and spiritual attributes previously dichotomized. The Romantic child defined children in terms of what adults were not: in Higonnet's words, "not sexual, not vicious, not ugly, not conscious, not damaged." The knowing child presents a less simple alternative. As Higonnet remarks, children are as much about "difficulty, trouble, and tension" as they are about "celebration, admiration, and passionate attachment." This confronts adults with "many more challenges as well as many more pleasures than any idea of childhood has done before."

This does not mean that there are not important distinctions between childhood and adulthood or that children are sexually, morally, or spiritually sophisticated or responsible. It means time has come to redefine the differences along new lines that do not rob children of sexual, moral, and spiritual knowledge and agency. Children do not yearn for innocence or carefree play to the extent that popular opinion romanticizes; nor are adults so sophisticated or superior.

The image of the knowing child suggests an acute awakening of moral and religious questions. Recent events such as school shootings and child-on-child violence have raised serious questions about how to judge children's moral and spiritual capacities and adult responsibility. Adults now question the modernist assumption that children naturally know what they need or are innately inclined to do good. How well do children really know what they want? Are their desires as susceptible as adult desires to the human temptation of wanting too much or wanting wrongly or destructively? As historian of religion Margaret Bendroth asks, "Can a child indeed choose to do evil?"

At the same time, the muddling of innocence and depravity reveals that children are all the more vulnerable. By picturing children as innocent, adults failed to take them seriously and often abused adult responsibility for earnest protection of children's physical, moral, and spiritual well-being. Adults can no longer avoid their obligation to oversee children's safety and development by surrounding themselves with pictures of cuddly, unblemished, blissful infants. Life with children is often less than ideal for adults; at the same time, the adult world is sometimes less than ideal for children. But even if children and adults do not always enjoy their common world, knowing children insist that adults do a better job sharing it.

In a word, a rich moral and religious complexity has returned along with the honesty and real ambiguity of children and parenting. If the premodern family portrayed the child as imperfectible in a fallen world and the modern world saw the child as perfectible in an imperfect world, the postmodern child is perhaps the most morally and spiritually perplexing: *the imperfect, even potentially volatile, child in an imperfect, volatile world.* We automatically react negatively to the idea of children as sinful or depraved, but the history of the "depraved adultish-child" of premodern times and the "innocent childish-child" of modern times has shown the limits of both views. The reign of the cherished, romanticized child created its own set of problems every bit as troubling as belief in the sinful, corrupt child had done. Both are inventions or social constructions in need of fresh reconsideration.

Complexifying children necessarily means a more complex view of how adults understand themselves as well. A society reorienting its bearings on what defines childhood also struggles with what it means to be an adult, what responsibilities and sacrifices adulthood entails. Historical and social trends demand new moral and religious competencies on the part of both adults and children. Both childhood and adulthood involve complicated combinations of all three categories of depravity, innocence, and knowledge. But these categories especially need to be rethought in relationship to children.

What does it mean to consider children as imperfect, even potentially volatile, in an imperfect, volatile world? Does it make a difference whether imperfection is understood in a material sense, as one would regard a defective product, or with greater moral and religious sensitivity that recognizes fallibility and the need for forbearance, leniency, pardon, charity, and spiritual growth?

Where should responsibility for human fallibility be placed? Can we retain a protected space for childhood without muddling it up with romanticized adult fantasies about purity, incompetence, and impotence? As important, the imperfectability and volatility of the world beg for adequate interpretation and reinterpretation in light of Christian understandings. How should Christians describe the world and the place of children within it? What do Christians tell children when they say that theirs is a certain kind of world?

If a major reinvention of childhood is under way—if innocence, guilt, and knowledge have surfaced as prominent categories of debate—then religion has a critical role to play. As cherished conventions of childhood are upset and competing images of children's and adults' responsibilities multiply, articulating a fresh Christian reading on children and child rearing becomes more than a purely academic exercise. It becomes a matter of contributing to a reinvention that is already in progress, and in need of a richer variety of perspectives, including ones that might address the moral and spiritual insights many secular approaches overlook.

Chapter 2

POPULAR PSYCHOLOGY

Children as Victims

———

If psychology has replaced religion in constructing the child, how do its perceptions measure up? A growing body of parenting literature fills bookstore shelves and receives lots of media attention. Books about the harm done to girls (such as Mary Pipher's *Reviving Ophelia*) or the difficulties of raising boys (such as Dan Kindlon and Michael Thompson's *Raising Cain*) quickly rise to the top of the best-seller list and make the circuit of television talk shows, newspaper interest stories, and daily conversation. Parents worry that their daughter's confidence will plummet when she reaches adolescence or that their son will adopt the "boy code" of emotional illiteracy, stoicism, and cruelty. Today's parenting generation has become increasingly psychologically sophisticated. Yet are children and parents any better off than previous generations as a result? What kind of moral and spiritual framework for understanding children does psychology provide?

PICKING ON PSYCHOLOGY FOR CHILDREN'S SAKE?

———

Suddenly, *therapeutic*—a term that suggests healing—has become a bad word. Conservatives and neoliberals alike tack this adjective on to any politics or movement that they want to discredit as promoting selfishness and loose morals. Psychology stands accused of promoting the "me generation," a self-centered view of life in which individuals care only about personal fulfillment. Hand in hand with "therapeutic liberalism" and "therapeutic individualism," psychology has, many critics say, corrupted the American commitment to the wider social good.

Criticism grows particularly heated when it comes to the subject of families. In an editorial introduction to a recent issue of *Theology Today* on children, Ellen Charry casually rules out psychology. "Self-realization psychology," as she calls it, "lacks the sources for a self-concept that can endure through danger and hardship, and honor the dignity of sacrifice for a greater good." Psychology simply promotes the shortsighted goal of wanting "children to feel good about themselves." Others say churches have uncritically aligned themselves with a therapeutic ethic that indiscriminately endorses sexual liberties and crowds out substantive discussion of family commitments.

Psychology, it seems, has also paved the way for rising singleness, childlessness, and single parenting. Spouses no longer tolerate personal unhappiness and seek divorce at the drop of a hat. Moreover, the helping professions are said to undermine parental authority and confidence by persuading parents to look to experts instead of relying on their own knowledge and local community.

Some of this concern is warranted. Parents who regularly put their own needs before those of children cause children to suffer. Adults guided by psychology alone cannot prepare children for the strenuous challenges of moral and religious development. If a parent knows how to increase a child's self-esteem but finds it a struggle to discuss such spiritual matters as prayer or human fallibility, a child may not have a way to talk about the desire for God or to anguish over harm done. Wholesale adoption of psychology has meant that fewer people look to specifically Christian resources for moral or religious guidance.

When it comes to children, however, such blanket dismissal of psychology is premature. If any discipline has given children a fresh voice and special place, it is psychology. Freud, in fact, got everyone's attention precisely because he argued for the importance of childhood. His theories were scandalous not just because he talked about sexuality but because he talked about sexual desire *in childhood*. He studied adults, but he dared to suggest that these adults had important emotional needs when they were children, needs that adults should take more seriously. Adults do not simply leave childhood behind. What happens to children is significant and deserves our utmost attention.

Children as Victims

Later analysts and psychologists, from Freud's own daughter, Anna, to Robert Coles, took up this mission with a vengeance. Where Freud reconstructed childhood largely from the adult perspective of free associations, dreams, and memories, others began to consider children in and of themselves, and not just as a place where adult pathology first develops. Ironically, the study of children became a respectable science at about the same time that interest in children seems to have waned among Christian scholars.

Turning therapeutic into a bad trait simply marks a new twist in a long-standing history of religious antagonism toward psychology's view of religion as an illusory (or even delusional) wish fulfillment and neurosis at the start of the twentieth century. But at the level of lived practice, public intellectuals have been unable to squelch psychology's appeal. From Freud's monumental *Interpretation of Dreams* at the turn of the twentieth century to Transactional Analysis ditties of "I'm OK, you're OK" in the 1970s, modern psychology has proven itself quite capable of providing a fresh way to understand human problems, understandings that Christianity had seemingly ceased to offer. Intellectual elites may criticize psychology, changing over time only in tack and tone, but the general public's appetite has continued unabated.

Psychology has extended to children what Freud suggested as a rich counseling technique: "closely hovering attention." Therapeutic and psychological attention hovers over children, listening closely to them and their words (spoken and unspoken), and then goes back again, and once again, to ask what one has missed. This is precisely what Anna Freud recommends when Robert Coles wonders where to go after his five-volume work on children in crisis. Go back over your work and see what you have missed, she says. So he went back over his field notes and made the rich discoveries that led to his best-selling trilogy on the moral, political, and spiritual lives of children.

Although self-identity should not be fashioned completely around self-realization psychology, psychology does tell us a great deal about how healthy and dysfunctional selves develop, how children perceive themselves, and how adults perceived themselves in childhood. One can, for example, debate theologically whether or not the family ought to act as "a little church." But from a psychological perspective, the family unavoidably creates an initial foundation for faith. The question then becomes not *whether* the family is a little church but *how well* families function in this capacity. In understanding such questions, psychology can be of immense assistance.

By definition, psychology as a discipline focuses on the individual. But this does not mean that all psychology advocates personal self-gratification. Some psychologists advance other goals besides self-fulfillment that are quite similar to the Golden Rule. Healthy self-development is seen as mutually dependent upon one's ability to help others develop. Even psychoanalytic theorists, who continue to focus on the inner world of the psyche, have begun to define child development relationally rather than individualistically. The psyche is not a seething cauldron of sexual and aggressive desires battling against society but an ill-formed self, yearning for and dependent upon the quality of its relationships. Children do not, then, move from dependence on significant others to independence but rather from immature to more mature connections. Nor does psychology's focus on the individual force therapists in the clinical setting to ignore a counselee's commitments to others. Many counselors operate with what might be called an ethic of connection or relationship. Good therapy guided by this ethic tries to give people the emotional sophistication to sustain relationships in a highly complex society, not to neglect them.

In other words, unthinking dismissal of psychology is problematic. Psychology is one of the most prevalent voices shaping contemporary views of children. People need a broader perspective from which to judge its enormous informational output. In particular, as we will explore in a moment, it has indicted parents on several counts. A key question then becomes, How do the religiously minded of all faiths, and Christians in particular, situate psychology and its charges in a broader scheme of life that includes religious understandings of human will and destiny?

CHILDREN AS VICTIMS OF NARCISSISTICALLY NEEDY PARENTS

The plot of Alice Miller's best-selling book *The Drama of the Gifted Child* seemed like every person's storyline when the book first appeared in Europe in 1979 and then in the

United States in 1981. The idea that needy parents push children to repress their own desires in order to meet their parents' needs hit a raw nerve. Miller herself believes that she touched something universal. Many people, she says, trace their "personal awakening" to her book.

The scenario of parental disregard and loss of self begins innocently enough. A toddler desires and reaches for a parent's ice cream cone. Believing that the child cannot handle a cone, the parent offers only a small spoonful. In frustration, the child whines. Again the parent refuses. The child cries, tries again, sobs, grows disheartened. Disconcerted, perhaps even angered, the adult scolds the child. Or amused, the adult laughs and tries to humor the child.

In either case, the result is the same. Narcissistically immature parents fail to respect the child as the person she or he is at any given time and the child loses a sense of herself or himself. Here *respect* refers to a variety of receptive attitudes toward children: to take seriously, admire, follow, regard with awareness, understand, tolerate, mirror, or reflect back feelings. Whining must stop, regardless of its merit, because the mother cannot tolerate the anxiety it provokes. Or a child must excel in school or competitive sports because the father needs the emotional gratification of the success of the child with whom he has merged. When a parent repeatedly fails to respect a child by refusing to tolerate the child's emotional responses or by seeking gratification through the child's achievements, the child perceives herself as fundamentally untrustworthy. Rather than recognizing feelings—anger, jealousy, anxiety, and grief—as integral parts of the self, children subvert such feelings to keep their parents happy.

"Gifted" children who have unusually powerful emotional antennas are the most prone to harm. They learn quickly how to read and meet the parent's inner needs, forfeiting their own desires and, in essence, their own selves in order to be loved. Such children experience a double hit. The parent is not available to meet the child's primary needs for understanding and the child feels compelled to meet the parent's needs at the cost of the child's self. As a result, the child is unable to experience consciously certain internal emotions, develops an "as-if personality" or "false self" that is based on responses to parental needs, and remains dependent on approval. Such a child may develop intellectual capacities but not the world of emotions and will grow into an adult who must seek greater and greater accomplishments to counter an underlying sense of worthlessness.

Emotionally deprived children go on to become parents who use their children to get the self-affirmation missing in their own childhood. That is, parents do to children what was done to them. This prediction actually echoes the old Hebraic saying that the iniquity of the fathers is visited "upon the children and the children's children, to the third and the fourth generation" (Exod. 34:7).

In later publications and editions of the initial volume, Miller became angrier and more strident, and she eventually rejected psychoanalysis itself. In the early 1980s, around the time that child abuse began to receive much public attention, she wrote less about parental narcissism and more about intentional cruelty and physical abuse. The child suffers not only from emotional humiliation but also from corporal punishment and sexual violation. Miller describes in increasingly horrifying detail what she calls "poisonous pedagogy," the cruel mental and physical techniques used by parents and teachers to squelch the spontaneity and vitality of children. By 1988, convinced that psychoanalysis itself had joined others in hiding the real abuse suffered by children, Miller resigned from the Swiss and international psychoanalytical associations. However we evaluate Miller's ideas—a matter to which we will return after running through two other charges she spawned—she sounds a clear indictment of parents that deserves a serious hearing.

Children as Victims of a Girl-Poisoning, Boy-Fearing Culture

Several recent best-selling books have turned the lament about the damage caused by narcissistic or abusive parents into a tirade against our girl-poisoning, boy-fearing culture. If Miller makes parents into the enemy, these texts turn on U.S. society and accuse it of "cultural abuse." Miller's influence is evident. The author of one of the best known texts is Mary Pipher, who describes *Reviving Ophelia* as a natural outgrowth of Miller's work, putting the difference bluntly: "Whereas Miller sees the parents as responsible . . . , I see the culture as splitting adolescent girls into true and false selves." Families are not dysfunctional, she says. Culture is.

Media of every kind—movies, music, television, advertising—broadcast the expectation that girls be beautiful and sexual. Girls rapidly pick up these ideas and use them as standards to judge harshly both themselves and their peers. Pipher actually popularizes the more academic writings of educational psychologist Carol Gilligan. Gilligan began to study adolescent girls when she became troubled by her observation that bright, exuberant ten- and eleven-year-old girls "go underground" when they become adolescents, losing confidence in all that they knew and assumed about themselves. When they witness women without power in the wider public world and experience daily harassment, they become silent and deferential, and they begin the long and sorry road of defining themselves no longer around their own desires and gifts but around gaining approval and meeting the needs of others.

Pipher quietly carries forward Gilligan's protest against the largely male-dominated world of developmental studies. Until recently, well-known psychologists made men the primary subject of study and the standard by which women were defined. Although Pipher never says so, her book is a kind of liberation psychology for girls. Girls are oppressed by their very own "problem with no name." As in the feminist adage that the personal is political, eating disorders, suicidal ideation, self-mutilation, early sexual activity, and running away from home are more than personal. These problems result from living in a "junk culture."

Years have passed since the classic Broverman study of gender bias in clinical therapy documented a conflict for women between being women and being adults. Traits recognized as characteristic of healthy women, such as being caring or emotional, were not the same traits identified with healthy adults, such as being in control or asserting authority. Yet girls are still divided against themselves. They cannot be both female and vibrant, self-directed human beings. The contradictory messages run like this: "Be sexy, but not sexual. Be honest, but don't hurt anyone's feelings. Be independent, but be nice. Be smart, but not so smart that you threaten boys."

Not surprisingly, authors of several best-selling books on boys have recently jumped on the bandwagon, using a similar kind of analysis and benefiting from Pipher's book endorsement. The cause for alarm is familiar: increased risk of depression, loneliness, suicide, violence, and alcohol and drug use. But boys are silenced in different ways and for different reasons. A boy code that determines when one is a "real boy" demands stoicism; bravado; and denial of genuine feelings of fear, uncertainty, and emotional need. This culturally imposed emotional suppression, illiteracy, and isolation leads to self-denigration, and in turn to ridicule, teasing, taunting, ostracizing, and even emotional and sometimes physical harassment of other boys. A disturbing "culture of cruelty" is said to pervade schools and peer relationships. Rigid ideals of masculinity require boys to either assert power or be labeled a weakling.

Even though authors stress that this is not a diatribe against girls, the mistreatment of boys is repeatedly

Children as Victims

illustrated by contrast with the better treatment of girls. Parents encourage conversations about feelings with girls, not boys; the early school environment and its emphasis on reading and sitting still discourages boys more than girls; public discussion of fairness in education focuses on girls more than boys; boys suffer harsher physical and verbal discipline than girls; boys are nine times more likely to be diagnosed with attention deficit disorder. Some authors even urge parents to spend special time with boys in particular because they are indisputably the most undernurtured group. Such assertions can hardly help but return us to an age-old competition over seemingly limited parental and social goods.

When these clinicians turn on culture, they carry Miller's critique to a new level. They do not diagnose patients; they diagnose culture. They demand modifications in how culture constructs girls and boys. Culture, not so much parents, does a bad job defining "real" boys and girls. New norms and traditions are needed.

CHILDREN AS VICTIMS OF A PUNITIVE CHRISTIANITY

Psychology's indictments of parents and culture also indict Christianity, both directly and indirectly. Poisonous pedagogy, in Miller's opinion, is rooted in the Jewish and Christian traditions, encouraged by Christian child-rearing manuals, and perpetuated in Protestant homes. Others have taken up the baton and spelled out ways in which

Christian theology reinforces abuse. These accusations have had a vast impact on society and Christian ministry that has not really been measured or evaluated.

In one of the first and most important Miller-inspired explorations, historian Philip Greven is clear about the religious roots of punishment: "The most enduring and influential source for the widespread practice of physical punishment . . . has been the Bible." Several passages in the Book of Proverbs offer the most direct instruction on use of the rod (for example, "Those who spare the rod hate their children, but those who love them are diligent to discipline them"; Prov. 13:24). Another key text in the Letter to the Hebrews exhorts parents to chastise their children as the "'Lord disciplines those whom he loves'" (Heb. 12:6). More troubling is the general portrayal in both Testaments of a God who requires obedience unto death, in asking Abraham to sacrifice his son, and then in commanding the crucifixion of God's own son. The German manuals quoted at length in one of Miller's books offer biblical warrant for a godlike parental authority and a child's duty of unquestioning obedience. If God chastises those who wander away, runs the argument, so also must parents.

From the seventeenth century to the present, these motifs have seeped into U.S. parenting through evangelical child-rearing guides that say teaching obedience requires inflicting pain. Even though moderate Christians may find the idea of breaking a child's will through physical punishment more abhorrent than evangelicals do, believing that aggression only begets more violence, they still see physical discipline as a last resort when all else has failed. But bending the will, in Greven's opinion, is not much better than breaking it, for both continue a history of religious justification of force and punishment.

These accusations found an immediate audience in the last decade among feminist and pastoral theologians. Religious beliefs not only legitimate physical punishment, many argue; some religious ideas are inherently traumatizing. Fears about sin, unworthiness, and condemnation bother children in ways adults often overlook. Particularly appalling is the traditional view that God is responsible for Jesus' suffering and sacrifice on the cross. This depiction of "divine" or "cosmic child abuse," as some have named it, wrongly exalts suffering and paves the way for parental mistreatment. God condones and even requires suffering as essential to salvation. Some even believe that theologians who have suffered harm as children in turn create distorted and destructive religious doctrines. Miller's groundbreaking work stands in the background behind these accusations.

RESPECTING A CHILD'S NEEDS: PSYCHOLOGY CORRECTS CHRISTIANITY

How are parents to assess these forceful charges of parental, cultural, and Christian damage? First, why are these premises so powerful? And then where do they finally go astray?

Theologians such as Charry complain that psychology lacks the resources for building a self-concept that can "endure hardship and sustain sacrifice." But this is not entirely true. Psychology begins with the fundamental question of children's needs and in many cases has helped adults see children anew. Fresh explanations of an infant's need for soothing or for facial expression and verbal contact, for example, can help parents go the extra mile. Reminders that adolescents are prone to self-absorption or parental ridicule as they search for their own identity allow parents to back off and suspend their knowing criticism. Helping parents understand why children do what they do sounds simple, but experience proves that adults have made grievous errors in their perceptions. Psychology's practiced ability to comprehend children's thought processes and behaviors makes it profoundly important to anyone who cares about children.

Psychology insists that adults take the child's point of view. In fact, the most important trait of good parenting, according to most psychologies, is to learn from children. Learning from children is extremely difficult, something that some people compare to a kind of religious practice, like meditation or Zen (an idea to which I will return). Psychology, like religion, sometimes sums it up with the term "love." The epigraph of the last chapter in *Raising Cain* (on "What Boys Need") is a quote from object relations theorist D. W. Winnicott, simply answering that a child "absolutely needs to live in a circle of love."

What exactly does providing a circle of love entail from a psychological vantage point? How does it challenge or correct traditional Christian conceptions? Miller is adamant: a child's most basic emotional need is for "respect, echoing, understanding, sympathy, and mirroring." Here, more than she acknowledges, Miller is influenced by the self psychology of psychoanalyst Heinz Kohut, and both of them show the stamp of other theorists, such as Winnicott. How much did Christian assumptions that circulated in the surrounding culture influence all of them? However one answers this, there is no doubt that these theorists made major strides in extending to children religious views about love and inherent human self-worth.

Three generations removed from Freud, both Winnicott on British soil and Kohut on American gradually strayed from traditional psychoanalytic emphasis on instinctual striving and oedipal conflict and began to attend to the relational needs and desires of early pre-oedipal stages of childhood. Kohut's writings on the self are replete with easy-to-picture sketches of undeniable human desires and heartaches. A lot of ink has been spilled on Kohut's implications for counseling, but few people have suggested ramifications for raising children. It is a natural next step. In my own clinical training, I thought I was learning about Kohut's theories to use them in counseling, but where they really had an impact was on my own life as a new mother. His self psychology forced me to consider important questions. What is a parent's job description? What is really needed in childhood?

Trained in psychoanalysis in the late 1940s, Kohut became progressively disenchanted with classic analytic

LET THE CHILDREN COME

explanations of human pathology. The people who made their way to his office were no longer struggling with the obsessive-compulsive or hysterical symptoms that Freud saw. Clients complained instead about feelings of shame, rage, depression, and emptiness. They seemed extremely sensitive to failure and suffered wide swings in self-esteem, ranging from grandiose visions of self-importance to morbid, derogatory self-condemnation. Seemingly well-adjusted people evidently lacked parts of themselves that they looked for in others, including the therapist. Working his way backwards from these observations, Kohut hypothesized about the processes in early childhood by which the self is formed.

A child is born with at least two primary needs that must be met for healthy self-development. Kohut called these "narcissistic" needs not because they are inherently selfish or self-centered but because they are constitutive of a child's very earliest yearnings for selfhood. A child needs ideals, someone or something to admire, or something general to respect. A child also needs mirroring, a sort of inverse need to be admired and to feel special, or a sense of the parent's enthusiasm for the child—the "gleam in the mother's eye." When a parent functions as a reliable source of solace and encouragement, a child incorporates parental actions and images as an inner capacity or self-structure that eventually allows a child to soothe itself and discern its own ambitions, or to empathize with itself and establish ideals. Without such mirroring from and idealization of the parent, a child struggles to establish a sufficiently cohesive and enduring self.

Children as Victims

Here, as with so many contemporary psychologists who try to redefine childhood, Kohut and Miller stumble upon an age-old religious and moral debate about self-love and love of others. Although they do not frame their ideas in terms of the commandment to "love others as one has loved oneself," they essentially question how popular Christianity has understood love of others as requiring unconditional self-sacrifice and annihilation of self-love. Miller in particular responds to a German culture influenced by Lutheran views. The heart of Martin Luther's social ethics opposes self-love to love of others. One historian captures this powerfully in saying that for Luther "the Christian lives not for himself but for the benefit of others. And nowhere is this more apparent—and important—than in the God-ordained fortress of our common life, the Christian household." Loving others is set over against love of the self as if the two were mutually exclusive. Self-interest taints genuine love; real love completely conquers self-interest. Although theologians before and after Luther have debated this premise, it has nonetheless permeated popular piety far beyond particular denominational lines. Dominant streams of Christianity have as a rule disparaged narcissism, interpreting it simplistically to mean "to love oneself obsessively" or "to think of oneself too highly" or "to be egocentric." Many parents, fearful of a young child's characteristic egocentrism, refrain from indulging a child's enthusiastic, prideful exhibitions and expect her to put the needs of others before her own, sometimes at quite an early age, often before she has developed the emotional or mental capacity to do so.

Whether they realize it or not, Kohut and Miller build an interesting counter-psychological-moral argument to this Christian view: in contrast to Christian biases, there is such a thing as "healthy narcissism." Without healthy self-love established in life's early years, love of others is impossible. "A little reflection soon shows how inconceivable it is really to love others," Miller argues, "if one cannot love oneself as one really is. And how could a person do that if, from the beginning, he has had no chance to experience his true feelings and to learn to know himself?"

Contrary to both traditional psychoanalysis and Christianity, children and adults do not outgrow such narcissistic needs. Ideally, a child grows not just from (self-centered) love of self to the love of others but also from immature, primitive, archaic means of meeting narcissistic needs to a more mature self-regard. How a parent responds to narcissism's early fluctuation plants the seeds for important development in later life.

Under optimal conditions, dependence on progressively more mature and expansive means of meeting narcissistic needs evolves throughout life. From confident self-aggrandizement as a child come resources for ambition and accomplishment. From favorable idealization comes the capacity for sustained commitment and value-oriented behavior. So, for Kohut, the "way out" of narcissism is to "go back into it." That is, the way out of immature narcissism is to enter self-absorption, understand its genesis, and nurture its transformation into more mature forms, not through denial but through recognizing justified narcissistic needs.

The circle of love advocated by a child-respecting psychology understands that children disrupt, destroy, take, frighten, wear down, and wangle all as part of normal—not abnormal—development. Such love allows little wiggle room for justifying corporal punishment as being good for children on the basis of Christian principles. Paddling does not, as some try to argue, promote civil behavior; just the opposite. New regard for children refutes accepted "truths" of conventional pedagogy as destructive to both children and parents: that strong feelings are dangerous, that a child's will must be broken, that tenderness is harmful and order and strictness are good for children, that thinking less of oneself fosters altruism. Contemporary psychology has successfully asserted fresh truths that even conservative churches now use to couch their directives about using the rod: genuine discipline occurs in a context of love, it should not crush or kill the spirit with harsh or brutal force, and it is never an excuse for abuse.

When we turn from the indictment of parents to the cultural indictment in Pipher and others, Christianity is challenged more by omission than commission. Pipher and others want to change how culture regards real boys and girls while almost completely ignoring religion. They come up with a variety of stop-gap measures but say strikingly little about faith and faith communities. Pipher recommends centering as an absolutely fundamental skill for girls; others call for nourishing boys' internal life, but this retrieval of a quiet time focused on one's inner feelings and thoughts is detached from its natural religious connections. Congregations could make available so many of the components called for by these books besides the practice of centering: protected space, belief in a larger cause, support in times of adversity, affirmation of selfhood and responsible decision making, countercultural values and cultural critique, sexual guidelines, positive peer relations, intergenerational activities, the practice of altruism and honesty, and a balance of affection and structure as well as belonging and freedom. By and large, these authors assume that religion has little power to help teens or to inform and change culture. Do congregations no longer offer protected space, alternative values and practices, or support for parents?

Perhaps these psychologists are worried that religious talk, even if not confessional, would dampen a book's popularity or public reach. Or, less speculatively, they have likely been trained, as most psychologists are, simply to disregard or discount religious beliefs and practices as not relevant or even harmful. Pipher says she was a "loyal Methodist" at thirteen, and a disenchanted questioner at fifteen, but apart from a few quick anecdotes of teens finding comfort in religious causes she drops the discussion. Many psychologists are all too aware of how congregations have accepted misogyny, failed girls, and hidden sexual abuse by family and clergy. Regardless of the reason, most psychologists fully accept religion's privatization. By completely avoiding the issue, however, these authors bring us back to a question that drives this book: Can Christianity make any difference in how people understand and seek to empower girls and boys today?

Children as Victims

SHAPING A CHILD'S NEEDS:
CHRISTIANITY CORRECTS PSYCHOLOGY

———

Psychology offers a powerful corrective to Christian views of children. But where do its indictments of parents, culture, and Christianity ultimately go astray? Few theologians have questioned Miller's influential framework. Psychological ideas are so compelling that many people consume them unquestioningly. Greven, for example, simply admits that Miller's books became a "part of my internal world, so thoroughly have I absorbed them."

Questioning Miller is a risky venture. Child misuse and abuse in the name of Christian love is a real and serious problem. Putting this problem on the table has not been easy. I do not want to lessen the pressure on theologians and parents alike to consider the damage done to children (not to mention its religious justification). Religious people of all persuasions must be more careful when they admire Abraham's faith in offering up Isaac; argue for the importance of a wrathful, judging God; glorify Christian sacrifice; interpret the central act of communion only in terms of God's sacrifice; and counsel children on the virtues of humility, forsaking self, and walking the way of the cross. These ideas have a place in doctrinal ruminations, but in daily practice they have all too often served to justify cruel treatment of children. Theologians must assume greater responsibility than they have so far for the distortion of their formal proclamations in everyday faith. These distortions undermine theology's lofty goals.

Questioning Miller is a risky venture for more personal reasons. Any such critique must consider its ulterior motives. Am I simply taking my parents' side and resisting the truth about my own childhood? This is precisely the pattern of destructive pedagogy that Miller predicts: one will go to great lengths to preserve parental innocence and love. I, however, have read Miller not only as an adult remembering my childhood (the audience she really has in mind) but also as a parent and a Christian (an audience for which she does not care much). From this perspective, I must ask, What are the limits and problems with her psychological diagnosis of human nature and responsibility?

Psychologists are amazingly confident in therapy's ability to cure human ailments and often judgmental and uninformed about the role of religion. Childhood mistreatment and its repression is often seen as the root cause of every disorder, and for Miller as the source of evil in the world. Emotional expression is the principal remedy. One must fully experience repressed feelings; mere talk does not suffice. Nor, in Miller's words, do "preaching forgiveness, discipline, goodwill, and 'spirituality'" because they simply cover over the pain. Rather, therapy involves accepting the truth about one's destructive childhood and rediscovering one's own naturally good "true self." Religion is only necessary, she remarks, when "real procedures," that is, therapeutic interventions, are lacking.

The culture-blaming books are similar. Shaped more by cognitive behaviorist than psychoanalytic theory, they advise a kind of damage control. Parents need to recognize the damage culture does and offer shelter from the storm through new coping strategies. Therapy functions as "emergency rescue work" with concrete steps girls can take to get their lives back under their own control. Pipher's book is all about consciousness raising. The solution in the boy books is comparable: a psychologically reeducated public, particularly parents, must expand boys' emotional vocabulary. Down-to-earth techniques—being direct, modeling emotions, creating daily rituals for protected space to talk—will help boys discern their own true selves.

Yet there are problems with these strictly psychological diagnoses and remedies. To begin to state the issues in terms of the example of the child and the ice cream cone: What if the child in fury hits the offered spoon of ice cream across the room, bites another child, or threatens her own safety? What if this has happened not once but many times? Must parents meet every narcissistic need without fail? Is there any allowance for parental exhaustion, or for learning from genuine and inevitable mistakes?

Here Kohut and Winnicott propose a helpful psychological correction to Miller and her cohorts. Where psychology often longs for perfect parents or a perfect culture, Kohut and Winnicott build failure into their understanding of development, therapy, and parenting. Kohut likens empathy (or the capacity to think and feel oneself into the inner life of a child) to oxygen, so fundamental is it to development. Yet negotiating empathic failures or "breaks" is equally important. Failure in parental empathy is to be expected; in fact, when not traumatic, it is the seedbed of growth. Parental failing sparks the very creation of internal self-structure in the child. When nontraumatic failure occurs, the infant must work to incorporate the missing function served by the idealized parent or the grandiose self—what parents provided in responding to the child's needs for idealization and mirroring—into the self's structure in transmuted or changed form.

Winnicott suggests the image of the "good enough" mother to capture a range of parental behavior that is less than ideal but adequate. A good-enough parent is sufficiently attentive on the one hand but avoids overindulgence and overprotection on the other hand. Like other ideals, even this one is capable of its own degeneration: Winnicott himself sometimes uses the term to describe a mother who is uncannily perfect in her responses. Nonetheless, both Winnicott and Kohut still consider disappointment, failure, and disillusionment essential elements in healthy development.

Nor is empathy equated without remainder with kindness, sympathy, warmth, permissiveness, and unconditional positive regard. Sometimes the most empathic response, the one most in tune with the child's narcissistic need for admiration and idealization, is correction, confrontation, and the setting of clear boundaries. So, in the incident of the child's desire for ice cream, the most empathic response may not always be simply to give the child a cone.

This is good as far as it goes, but it still leaves unanswered important moral and religious questions. How does a parent discern the empathic response when the desire is not an ice cream cone but something more complex and ambiguous, as most human desires become over the years? Does desire ever need to be curbed? Can parents and society love children without faltering? Is there any place for teaching children and youths not to think only of themselves and to care for others?

If Christian theology has erred on the side of moral mastery and condemnation, psychology errs on the side of moral naïveté. Miller contends that "a child who has been allowed to be egoistic, greedy, and asocial long enough will develop spontaneous pleasure in sharing and giving." Certainly, children pushed too soon to love others out of duty will fail to develop adequate resources to do so. But altruism and many other virtues seldom emerge as spontaneously as these psychologies imagine. In a word, sometimes a child's needs must be shaped and formed rather than always simply met.

When Kindlon and Thompson attempt to interpret the biblical story behind their book title (*Raising Cain*), they illustrate vividly psychology's tendency to underestimate the human capacity for wrongdoing. "How different Cain's story might have been," they presume, "had he been able to draw upon inner resources, emotional awareness, empathy, and moral courage." They believe the problem is not human proclivity toward evil but inward emotional confusion. A more emotionally astute Cain, helped to understand his inner life by sensitive parents and a culture with a wider range of male role models, would not have killed Abel. All human beings, they believe, are naturally motivated to be better than they are. As a result, Kindlon and Thompson miss the complex dynamic that the biblical writer had in mind. Seeing Cain's distress, the Lord warns him sin is "lurking at the door; its desire is for you, but you must master it" (Gen. 4:7). Human nature is so much more complex in this religious view, with sin and evil a challenge, and even a threat, that humans must take seriously and face with courage and audacity before they overpower us.

For the most part, psychology sympathizes with children but has little regard for their complicated nature and the ambiguities of parenting. Concern that children not be held responsible for inappropriate and destructive adult behavior has led to extraordinary restraint surrounding (and even avoidance of) the topic of childhood and "sin," a Christian word for human alienation and brokenness. With the arrival of the Enlightenment and modern science, many people followed modern theologians who gave up the idea of original sin as an inherited taint of all children since Adam and Eve. Psychological efforts to figure out why children turn out the way they do, as we saw in the last chapter, displaced debate about innocence and sinfulness with endless quarrels about the role of nature and nurture. When children struggle and fail to thrive, psychology mostly blames parents and society, picturing children as victims.

As a result, psychology depicts children as more virtuous, dependent, and helpless than classic Christian readings do, sometimes to the extreme of identifying parents (either unempathic mothers or abusive fathers) or girl-poisoning and boy-fearing culture as the sole locus of evil and wrongdoing. Ironically, in this effort to give children power, psychology actually ends up robbing them of moral agency by blaming the parent or culture exclusively; exaggerating the willful control of adults; and ignoring the complex dynamics of human failure, reconciliation, and hope.

Children have far less control over their actions than adults, and blame often lies rightfully on the parent's doorstep. But they still have some control. Children can act perversely of their own human and God-given volition. Debunking the myth of innocence in children requires gaining greater knowledge about good and evil in others, children and adults alike. Moral and religious development actually requires gaining control and discernment with age. This does not come easily or even naturally. Moreover, adults have a responsibility to curb children's harmful, aggressive, and inhumane desires—and, more difficult yet, to model love of self, neighbor, and God. Most parental discipline lies precisely in the gray area between appropriate attempts to address genuine misbehavior or shape good behavior and destructive abuse of children.

Caution about sin has also resulted in an inability to recognize inevitable human frailty and, consequently, the need for reprieve or grace. Or, as one of my parent friends said, "For people who grew up around heavy sin language, caution makes sense. But at some point, some things are just wrong." Given human frailty, children will go astray and adults will inevitably fail children. Parents may harm children not because they were harmed as children, as many psychologists claim, but in a moment of temper gone awry, out of control, or on an impulse that sometimes has no other name than evil. Likewise, society harms children when it willingly and knowingly fails to arrest the forces that have a destructive effect. This is not to excuse adult or cultural misbehavior but to put it into a more complicated religious and moral context.

Spiritual allowance for human frailty and broken-ness is an essential part of good parenting. So many contemporary manuals on child rearing, shaped by psychology's overriding optimism, fail to recognize this. Miller, for example, recommends that a parent who hits a child in an attempt at discipline should admit that the child was slapped out of confusion and not out of love. But curiously enough, she pays little heed to the huge question of where parents find the resources for such gestures of admission and confession. She even ridicules religious efforts to teach about the practice of forgiveness. However, genuine repentance and even the ability to apologize involve rigorous moral and religious disciplines of self-examination and circumspection that have been better developed by religion than by contemporary psychology. This is true even if the rituals and practices that help families enact Christian ideals of repentance, forgiveness, reconciliation, and hope (such as prayer, confession, worship, storytelling, and religious discussion) are precisely the practices that have not weathered well the storms of modernity. In the end, however, genuine reconciliation depends not so much on right rituals or Christian beliefs, for in Christianity it is not something humans can entirely control or will into being but instead something that ultimately rests on grace.

Appreciating the brokenness of parents and children ironically makes both parties more accountable. Mothers and fathers must accept responsibility for actions that do not entirely originate in an abusive childhood. Optimally, children must gradually assume greater accountability for actions and feelings in relationship to others that are not wholly caused by unsympathetic or abusive parents or a hostile culture. Eventually adults must curb their own ongoing narcissistic needs to be loved in order to care genuinely for a child, an effort that sometimes demands sacrifice of one's own desires.

In short, children's needs and desires must be more than simply respected; they must be shaped. Christianity may not have done such a great job on this, but at least it has broached the questions. Understanding human brokenness and reparation is crucial to understanding the difficult dynamics of child rearing. Without appreciation for human sin and grace, the nuances of a child's moral and religious development become lifeless and vacuous. The tendency to attribute evil to either heredity or the environment robs the child of responsibility, will, and freedom; overlooks the complexity of parenting; and ignores the richness of religious traditions that have attempted to understand human frailty and grace.

Although Miller overtly rejects Christian views of formation, covertly she advocates important values that she likely absorbed from the same Christian culture she casts off. This is clear when she defines her ultimate goal at the beginning of her second book, *For Your Own Good:* "I imagine that someday we will regard our children not as creatures to manipulate or to change but rather as messengers from a world we once deeply knew, . . . who can reveal to us more about the true secrets of life. . . . We do not need to be told whether to be strict or permissive with our children. What we do need is to have respect for their needs, their feelings, and their individuality, as well as for our own."

Three fundamental Christian imperatives lie behind these words, imperatives to which we return in the next few chapters. First, children must be loved for their own sake. Christians, however, argue that parents and others can love children in this way only to the extent that we trust ourselves to have already been abundantly loved, so much so that we have what we need and want. Whereas Miller believes this love comes from parents, Christians see it as a gift, a grace ultimately promised and bestowed by God. Second, children must be received as harbingers of God's kingdom. In the midst of chaos, confusion, and problems, they do point to life's secrets. Finally, to cause a child to stumble and fall is a fate worse than death.

This is a rudimentary but wonderful foundation upon which to build. There is more constructive work ahead. Important and helpful Christian beliefs about children and Christian approaches to discipline besides punishment and obedience have been overlooked and deserve revival.

Chapter 3

CHRISTIAN FAITH

Children as Sinful

———

S everal decades have passed with little constructive
response to psychology's indictments. Influenced by
Alice Miller, Philip Greven mapped the ways in
which Christians justified harsh punishment of children
throughout the last four centuries of U.S. religion. Others developed these negatives into a fuller portrait, detail-
ing how Christians used Abraham's near-murder of Isaac,
Jesus as the ultimate sacrifice, and Hebrews 12:5–11 as a
warrant for rigid discipline of children. For many people,
Christianity stands rightfully accused of abuse.

Beyond the historical question of whether these portrayals are accurate or not, a key question goes unasked.
Can an alternative course on children and parenting be
drawn from the Bible and other Christian sources? If
"much Christian theology has been rooted in the threat of

punishment," as Greven contends, is there anything in the tradition worth salvaging? If uncompromising coercion, force, and spanking are not truly Christian—if they degrade, dehumanize, humiliate, and even breed public violence rather than inspire good behavior—doesn't theology need to get busy creating a more child-friendly picture of children?

Few people, to my knowledge, have done such work. In a volatile society, with children themselves involved in acts of aggression, crime, and murder, and with parents eager to find simple child-rearing solutions but becoming easy prey for those selling newly repackaged harsh disciplinary tactics, such questions are pressing. How are parents to view the moral and spiritual ambiguities of human fallibility in children? Do Christian understandings of sin and grace inherently lead to child abuse? Or can these doctrines be read in a fresh way to understand and empower children and parents?

ALTERNATIVE CHRISTIAN MANDATES: A MODEST BEGINNING

Greven actually suggests a bare-bones start. Nowhere, he emphasizes, does Jesus advocate physical punishment of children. Quite the contrary: he invites children in where others would put them out. He goes out of his way to heal their illnesses, says they embody the kingdom of God, and threatens eternal damnation to anyone who might harm their growing faith.

Other scholars who are justifiably concerned about child abuse and intolerant, rigid discipline, such as pastoral theologian Donald Capps, have also emphasized the Christian imperative to love children without harming them. Capps, in fact, develops a powerful theological case for grace toward children. The good news of the Christian gospel itself proclaims that adults and children alike are not banished forever from the Garden as a result of Adam and Eve's sin but instead given the promise of reprieve, return, reconciliation, and transformation.

However, this affirmation about the imperative to love children only appears briefly in these books, most often at the end of some lengthy argument reprimanding Christianity. It is hard to reconcile the hope that Christianity can support children with the pervasive worry that Christianity as Christianity is de facto predisposed toward "abusive theology," as pastoral theologian Stephen Pattison calls it. This criticism simply gets in the way of formulating a more child-friendly Christian view of children and better ways to raise them.

This whole discussion conducted by Greven, Capps, and Pattison gets stuck upon on a huge stumbling block in contemporary Christian theology and children: the relationship between grace and sin. Attributing sin to children has been used to justify inexcusably harsh treatment. For many, the only solution is to throw out Christian views of sin—or even Christianity entirely. Christians at least ought to quit dwelling on sin and start emphasizing the elated community in front of the empty tomb. But how realistic is skipping over sin and running straight for joy, given the human experience of failure and imperfection? Just as troubling, is this solution accountable to the larger Christian corpus that has, for centuries, struggled over questions of moral lapse and spiritual backsliding? Does this give adequate answer to those who continue to misuse the tradition to justify a narrowminded approach to raising children?

A more helpful and theologically responsible tack is to redefine sin, a project that Capps briefly takes up. Theological understanding of sin as rebellion against God is problematic. In such a view, rebellious children who defy their parents must be punished in order to learn obedience to parental and divine authority. They must learn at quite an early age the difference between right (parents' ideas) and wrong (children's ideas). This definition, however, fails to understand the whole of human brokenness. Sin is better understood to be alienation connected as much with shame as with guilt. Even before any act of disobedience, and certainly in its aftermath, children are insecure; fearful about their place before their parents' seemingly all-powerful prerogatives; hungry for adult confirmation of their value; and often, even in early childhood, instantly ashamed of going against known parental wishes. With shame, the problem runs deeper than guilt that "I did something wrong" to a sense that "I'm no good" or "I'm worthless" by standards both external and internal to the self. There are few actions one can take to rectify shame in the way that one can make up for guilt over bad behavior.

Such an understanding of sin suggests a different kind of parental response, though Capps does not develop this at any length. Children need patient, reliable recognition, appreciation, and understanding more than constant correction and penalty. As we have seen, this approach promotes the ideal of respect upheld most dramatically by modern psychology. In fact, the redefinition grows out of contemporary psychological views of shame and guilt more than from a serious reassessment of Christian claims. It does not, unfortunately, say much about the relationship between recognizing sin and raising children, or about the role of sin in children's development, whether sin involves shame or guilt. Nor does it address institutional or social forms of sin. Capps himself admits that he simply skips over the problem of how people might become better parents, disclaiming his own expertise, even though he believes that conservative Christian attempts have failed miserably. Readers cannot help but believe that he does know a thing or two about raising children. On the whole, however, books on abusive Christian theology focus on adults recovering from a difficult childhood and seldom on parents confronted with the challenges of parenting. They completely shy away from the far more difficult questions of understanding children when they are—as Capps admits they can be—deceitful, manipulative, and even malicious.

CHILDREN AS FALLIBLE

Years ago, by the lakeshore of a family summer camp, I shared a swing set with a couple of other eight- and nine-year-old girls. One of them said something about sin. I honestly had never really heard the word before. Granted, it might have been spoken during my regular attendance back home at the local Christian Church (Disciples of Christ) congregation in Indiana where I grew up. But the actual idea had not hit home yet. My new friend seemed equally amazed that the word was new to me. She apparently had to confess her sins regularly. Her depiction did not enlighten me. But a new awareness crept into my life. There was, I discovered in that early religious conversation, a word and a way to talk about betrayal of self, others, and God, an experience of faithlessness to which I was awakening. I had inadvertently stumbled upon a rather pivotal Christian theme.

I had, of course, survived just fine without knowing that. Indeed, a friend who grew up in a more conservative branch of the same nineteenth-century American-born revival movement from which my denomination sprang actually felt his own early religious hopes dashed and even damaged on the rock of overly harsh condemnation of sin in his household. This is so much the case for him and many like him that if they raise their children in the church at all, they seek out a progressive congregation where the topic may surface in weekly worship but is seldom mentioned in relationship to children themselves.

There is a sense that children do not need to hear about sin but also that they would not understand it if they did. In one study, a Catholic high school principal qualifies how she would respond to a student who steals something from a classmate. Her approach has gradually changed. Rather than resort to explicitly moral or religious language, including the language of sin, she prefers the pragmatic language of feelings ("How does it make you feel?" or "How would you feel?") or the utilitarian language of consequences ("You can't get away with this all your life"). Moral or religious language "would probably not relate to them anyway," she remarks. Such "symbols [of the faith] don't mean anything [to kids]," a youth minister at a large Presbyterian church in Chicago reports. The general feeling seems to be "We don't do sin," and "It isn't our thing."

Now, I do not make declarations that my children have sinned a common part of my parenting, either. Nor am I commending the practice, without a lot more qualification. But I want to give serious reconsideration to sin and grace in relation to children and parenting.

Augustine, the early-fifth-century theologian most responsible for formulating Christian views of original sin, saw its earliest appearance in the insatiable grasping of a well-fed infant at the breast. I did not see this when I nursed my sons, but I still am convinced that Augustine was onto something. Both my husband and I saw something akin to what Augustine described once a new baby brother entered our family (an observation with which Augustine would concur). He himself saw the infant's greed as provoked by jealousy in seeing another infant at the breast. Over the years, I have witnessed acts of meanness among my sons and their peers—a shabby spiritedness with which I identify and in which I have also caught myself—that seems to have no other obvious source besides the sheer pleasure of the shabby act itself. Connected to the pleasure is perhaps an unacknowledged but insidious self-disdain and a desire to feel better by making someone else feel worse. When a colleague recently told me about how her twenty-four-year-old son had acted out in completely irrational and potentially harmful ways, we half-joked about the relevance of the category of sin. Still, in all three instances—toddler, child, and youth—I would hesitate to make them an opportunity to lecture about the fall or redemption in Christ.

WHY JUMP INTO SIN?

Given the amazingly destructive role that doctrines of sin have ostensibly played in condoning abusive treatment of children, why jump into this thicket at all? Before amplifying the positive potential of this discussion by turning in the next section to specific illustrations in the Christian tradition, let me offer three general answers to this question.

First, as I have implied, there are resources in the Christian tradition to argue against the understanding of sin and children promoted by conservative Christians, and sometimes unfairly associated with Calvinist and Puritan so-called hellfire-and-damnation traditions. James Dobson, founder of Focus on the Family, is not the only Christian, nor will he be the last, to name the doctrine of sin as a reason for parental punishment. Failure to counter this view with alternative Christian interpretations has allowed people to misperceive this as the only Christian view of children and sin.

Not all allegations of evil in children are a form of religious contempt and abuse. In some cases, the ideas of original sin and redemption actually support more compassionate treatment of children in general. The social efforts and writings of eighteenth-century German Pietist August Hermann Francke are a nice instance of this. Understanding of sin actually motivated him to treat children with respect and kindness, as theologian Marcia Bunge documents, and, by leveling the playing field as one in which all are fallen, to extend such care to poor children in a deeply class-conscious society. Though perhaps less well known than Augustine, Francke is not alone in the history of the Christian tradition in his more positive treatment of doctrines of sin and children.

In a word, there is not a one-to-one correlation between ideas about original sin and harsh punishment of children. Historical notions of sin, grace, and children are far richer than conventional negative stereotypes. Major figures in Christian history, people often suspected as key culprits, have not in fact argued for severe discipline in response to sin in children. Augustine actually argues against physical reprimand; John Calvin does not advocate it; and even Jonathan Edwards, the notoriously fiery early-eighteenth-century preacher and theologian who calls children "young vipers," gives no instructions about breaking the will of sinful children. Without denying the harm their followers did in the name of each of these figures, the weight of the Christian tradition falls solidly in children's favor, as the rest of this and the next few chapters attempt to show.

Second, the history of the depraved adultish-child of premodern times and the innocent childish-child of modern times has shown the limits of both extremes. A more complex understanding of sin helps us move beyond the unfortunate dichotomy between children as wholly depraved and wholly innocent, villains and victims. It offers language with which to comprehend better the knowing children of today. It especially speaks to the moral and spiritual complexity of the teen years without pathologizing them. Contrary to the long-standing sentimentalized view of children as innocent and the more recent view of youth as especially troublesome, children and youths have valuable and increasingly complicated moral and spiritual lives. They do not occupy a religious or moral wilderness completely set aside from the adult world. Just as in my earliest childhood reckoning, the theological concept of sin gives children and adults a word and a way to talk about betrayal of self, others, and God, an experience that they undoubtedly have (and increasingly so as they grow).

Third, as this last statement implies, if one can talk about sin, restoration, and children, one can also talk about the intricacies of moral and spiritual development, a topic of serious concern for many pre-Enlightenment theologians but largely depleted of meaning today. Contrary to popular opinion, modern psychology did not invent life-cycle theories. Prior to modern views of children as innocent, many Christian theologians described the course of children's spiritual formation in relation to sin and grace in fruitful ways.

These largely forgotten understandings add something missing from more recent psychological views that freeze children in static childhood innocence and ignore complex moral and spiritual issues. Current life-cycle views divide life into psychological stages of either increasing independence or increasing relationality. The debate has centered around whether children move from merger with the primary caregiver to autonomy, or whether this ignores an infant's very early sense of separate selfhood and the need to move from primitive to more mature interdependence with intimate others rather than independence. Even theories of faith development in Christian education, where one might expect attention to dynamics of sin and grace, have dropped from the picture basic questions about the struggle with wrongdoing, evil, corruption, and reconciliation. The focus falls instead on generic stages of faith as involving an emotional and cognitive movement from the intuitive faith of young children through the conventional faith of youth to the self-transcending faith of those few who manage to reach the final stage of full maturity. When it comes to the serious moral and religious questions of contemporary child rearing, these are all enlightening but limited typologies.

By contrast, classical Christian developmental schemes capture important dimensions of children's evolving moral and spiritual struggle precisely in relationship to the dilemma of parental and communal nurture. They trace the dynamics of an incremental accretion of responsibility and make a place for human frailty, mistakes, destructive failures, and the need for amends and grace. These failures are not the occasion for despair or unrelenting guilt and shame but rather for deeper awakening, remorse, reparation, compassion, and formation. Knowing that humans are always predisposed to sin can give resources for resistance, forgiveness, and freedom. In contrast to the prevalent drive today to perfect children and parenting, this approach opens up space for a readier disclosure of shortcomings and the promise of reprieve. Talking about sin and grace can renew a sense of children's religious and moral potential, and moreover the obligation of adults for children's well-being, including the moral and spiritual. A Christian framework suggests that adults in a religious community have greater responsibility for children's formation than is usually assumed, including but going beyond their own biological offspring.

ILLUSTRATIONS FROM THE TRADITION

A stroll through the Christian tradition offers ample opportunity to illustrate these claims. Over history, theologians have worked hard to strike an appropriate balance between innocence and depravity, carefully qualifying and differentiating the terms *sin* and *innocence* in relationship to children and adults at different points in the life cycle. Two recent scholars, in fact, actually devise their own terms to capture the nuance with which important theologians—Augustine in early Christianity (A.D.

354–430) and Menno Simons as part of the Radical Reformation (1496–1561)—talked about children as sinful. In her work on Augustine, Martha Stortz suggests "noninnocence" as the best phrase to describe a third possibility that Augustine assumed between innocence and depravity, a position that others, such as Edwards, later adopt. In Augustine's eyes, an infant is willing but not yet capable of causing (nor strong enough to cause) harm, literally not harming, or "*in–nocens.*" In a similar fashion but for a quite different Christian figure and period, Keith Graber Miller invents the phrase "complex innocence" to capture Simons's understanding that children lack both bona fide adultlike sin and mature faithfulness. Children are more innocent than adults, but this is tempered by an inherited predisposition toward sinning that religious conversion and growth may correct. Both Augustine and Simons retain sin as a critical category, but they refuse any flat, fixed, one-size-fits-all definition.

We ought not, of course, skirt Augustine's highly ambiguous historical legacy. In the course of history, these same ideas lent themselves to justification of corporal punishment. In the very same volume as Stortz's argument for the subtleties of Augustine's view is another chapter that documents the harsh measures used by seventeenth-century Jesuit and Ursuline missionaries in their work among the Huron Indians in Canada. The missionaries imposed a physical discipline partly inspired by an Augustinian view of fallen human nature that was quite contrary to Indian affection for and indulgence of children. Augustine himself felt he had to argue that an

Children as Sinful

infant was tainted in the moment of conception itself, contaminated by Adam's semen, in order to foist off his religious opponents' optimistic claims about the ease with which humans could do good. That the infant was con-taminated in conception made infant baptism absolutely essential. This earnest rigidity about an infant's sinfulness grew out of Augustine's efforts to justify infant baptism more than out of a careful reading of biblical texts.

Still, Augustine's unusually close observations of children as well as his own personal struggles are fertile ground for wrestling with sin's manifestations. Sin is mis-directed, humanly unquenchable desire, a distorted de-sire that he believed evolves and deepens in stages as an infant grows to be a child, adolescent, and adult. Children are neither romanticized as wholly innocent, like Adam before the fall, nor completely beguiled by evil and in dire need of control, as some of his peers claimed.

Simons develops his own understanding of an inter-mediary position between innocence and guilt for almost opposite purposes, as part of a bigger argument *against* rather than for infant baptism. He also forged his view in opposition to enemies, those who accused him of murder-ing infants' souls by refusing to baptize them. In the process of providing scriptural, theological, and practical arguments for adult baptism, he distinguishes between being predisposed to sin and stepping into sin itself. Af-firming children's predilection to sin prevents adults from exaggerating children's guilelessness. Yet recognizing their initial distance from actual sin reminds everyone, children and adults alike, of a Christian's chief responsibility before

God. A child's complex innocence then entails an inborn impure nature that becomes a graver cause for concern only as a child acquires the ability to discern and confess human frailty. Until this moment arrives and baptism into faith is sought, a child is protected by Christ's grace and by the oversight of the Christian community. In contrast to Augustine, God's grace is efficacious enough and the community's role sufficient enough to cover all children until they reach a point of moral and spiritual discretion, a point in time Simons refused to specify absolutely.

Even though they differ in emphasis and ideal, parting ways over fundamental beliefs about baptism and religious community, both Augustine and Simons developed suggestive schemas to describe moral and spiritual development. Allowing for sin permitted them to describe the incremental moves from noninnocence or complex innocence to increased accountability and culpability. Although Simons did not believe that such maturity always coincided with chronological markers, he held that parents had a serious obligation to watch for, recognize, cultivate, and celebrate the age of accountability. Augustine, by contrast, drew on common understandings of antiquity to create a sophisticated demarcation of the changing nature of sin and accountability through six stages from infancy to old age, divided into seven-year intervals. Many who followed him— Aquinas, Luther, Calvin, and Edwards—composed variations on this same schema.

If an egotistic insatiability characterized the infant, Augustine proposed, disobedience is the notable sin of the second stage of life, in which children acquire language, perceive adult expectations, and learn the rules. In adolescence, infancy's noninnocence takes on an increasingly insidious form of deliberate malice, most characteristically exemplified for Augustine in his own youthful foray with friends into a fruit garden, stealing pears prompted by nothing else than the sheer delight of doing something wrong. This third development surpasses grasping desire or even outright disobedience because it does not just test but finally crosses over and assails the boundaries of basic human decency.

Even though Simons was reticent to delineate such developmental stages, other Anabaptists past and present do so. For some early Hutterites, childhood also unfolds in seven-year increments, with seven and fourteen the critical markers. But as with Simons, the religious community assumes an absolutely essential role. Religious rituals must sanction these turning points, and communal criteria for discipline must correspond to children's gradual ability to speak, understand, discern, and incorporate good habits and virtues.

Stortz actually names Augustine's developmental understanding as one of his major contributions to contemporary consideration of children. Of particular value is his grasp of the clear boundaries between the stages of life and his specification of chronologically appropriate levels of accountability. As she remarks, "Looking back on a gang-stealing of pears, Augustine lamented the sins of his youth—but at least he knew when it was over!" People in today's society, by contrast, dangerously and destructively blur the boundaries. Children, for example, are sometimes forced to grow up too soon, mimicking adult styles and sexual behavior or held up to legal penalties previously reserved for adults only, while adults fail to curb infantile pursuit of personal gratification at great cost to family and community. By contrast, Augustine understood development in terms of an increasing level of moral accountability. Although infants are not innocent by any means, it is silly and even wrong to rebuke them when they can neither understand nor reason. But with acquisition of language and cognitive ability comes greater accountability. Children who fail to obey verbal commands and adolescents who defy standards of human decency should face increasingly stiffer penalties. But neither group is as culpable as adults are. In Augustine's eyes, adults who prey upon children—whether making them assume adult responsibilities before they are ready or using children for their own ends in a variety of ways—have some serious moral and spiritual penalties to pay. In other words, the noninnocence of infancy, left unnoticed and untutored, is replicated, intensified, and amplified in the outright guilt of later stages of life. Adults deceive in ways children cannot fathom. In fact, centuries later, Luther will measure development precisely by sin's more flagrant appearance.

Yet in all this, adulthood and childhood are also deeply connected. Adults are grown-up children, "only more complex," as Stortz points out, with emphasis on both "children" and "grown-up." Ironically, children need the help of adults, who by the very nature of their age and maturity have the risk of greater fallibility but also the possibility of greater wisdom.

RAISING IMPERFECT CHILDREN
IN AN IMPERFECT WORLD

This foray into classic texts leads to several concluding observations. First, describing sin, virtue, accountability, and guilt in children is a daunting task, even if it contributes to enhanced understanding. Augustine, Simons, and other Christian theologians did so with fear and trepidation, as should we. The tension that surrounds this subject is epitomized in the Christian theology of Jonathan Edwards that arose during the eighteenth-century transition from viewing children as sinful to viewing them as innocent. Edwards preached what historian Catherine Brekus describes as a "double image of children." At one and the same time, they were tainted by sin and yet capable of a faith that could well surpass adult belief. As a result, he pummels them with fearful, anxiety-provoking accusations about their damnation. Yet he also had extraordinary respect for their moral and spiritual lives. For a time, in contrast to others of his era, he admitted converted children to full communion. He took them so seriously that he preached special children's sermons quite unlike the "charming" children's sermons of today. Although questionable in their focus on damnation and God's wrath, they nonetheless assume children had real minds and souls quite capable of dealing with deep existential worries and able to receive grace. If they were vipers, they were distinctly *young* vipers who had the chance before them of turning away from a more despicable adult version.

Naturally, Edwards's legacy is mixed. Many people have lamented that he perpetuated an abusive style of child rearing. Yet in asserting the category of sin as relevant, he represents a dying theological gasp for a more realistic, less sentimentalized view of children's imperfection in the face of an encroaching modernist ideology that proclaimed their purity and innocence. Precisely because he took the dynamics of grace and sin so seriously, he had immense regard for even young children's spirituality. Unfortunately, fear—one of the most favored motivators of Edwards and his Puritan predecessors—is probably among the worst human emotions to use as an incentive for good behavior. Earnest anxiety about children's precariousness and possible damnation led him to misuse threat as motivation for conversion.

Second, taking sin seriously gave adults greater responsibility in relationship to children. Despite stark differences in Augustine and Simons's understandings of children, sin, and baptism, the essence of parenting for these classical figures evolves around the spiritual and moral formation of children's beliefs, dispositions, and character. Moral and religious reasoning develops socially. A child cannot acquire appropriate self-determination without reasonable, faithful adults within a supportive community. As children gain responsibility as they age, parents have the difficult task of fine-tuning their attention to children's changing moral and religious capacity and welfare.

As this implies, hand in hand with claims about parental responsibility are huge assumptions about the social context and the critical role of collective rituals and believing communities in bringing children to religious commitment. A fertile fund of social resources is absolutely indispensable to development. For Augustine, only early baptism affords a genuine stay of execution in a world where evil is palpable and demons prevail; minimally, parents must provide for it. From a very different angle, Simon's emphasis on the Christian community's obligation to bring children to voluntary Christian commitment is one of his key contributions. Infant baptism misleads children and parents into a false sense of security that all the requirements have been met when many greater moral and spiritual hurdles still lie ahead. This view, as Keith Graber Miller puts it, "utterly obligated parents and the Christian community to nurture children" in the faith. In both cases, appreciation for sin suggests that parenting is a critical religious discipline and practice in its own right.

Ultimately, to end where we began, this exploration calls for a lively understanding of Christian discipline that departs significantly from more conservative Christian views. Although Focus on the Family has modified its claims about absolute obedience in recent years, perhaps in response to accusations of abuse such as Greven's, Dobson still believes that proper parental leadership means clear demonstration of authority of men over women and parents over children. In this and in claims about the necessity of corporal punishment, conservative Christians believe they have the Bible on their side. There are, however, strong grounds upon which to found alternative views.

Classic Christian statements on children and sin confirm a premise about discipline well captured by psychologist Bruno Bettelheim: that the "fundamental issue is not punishment at all but the development of morality—that is, the creation of conditions that not only allow but strongly induce a child to wish to be a moral, disciplined person." Criteria for discipline must correspond to a child's gradual maturation. Moreover, there is not a direct correspondence between sin and a need for punishment and control.

While contemporary liberal theologians deny expertise on children, it took this child psychologist to argue against the flat equation of discipline with punishment. Notably, he does so not just on psychological grounds but with reference to the gospel. The word *discipline* itself is integrally connected to Jesus' relationship with his disciples. The disciples follow him and open themselves to radical change because mutual love, trust, belief, and admiration draw them. Jesus' authority rests upon aligning himself with his disciples and not standing over them as commander-in-chief.

Discipline, then, has greater biblical affinity with teaching, guided by love and admiration, than with mastery, force, and chastisement driven by fear. Of course,

Bettelheim is not the first to say this. There are streams in the tradition, as we have seen, that have said as much. Other Christians have forbidden corporal punishment, even though they still expect children to obey their parents. Obedience, however, means adherence and alliance rather than deference and compliance and evolves from cultivating a desire for the good through example, education, family worship, and Bible study, not from setting up a system of external rewards and penalties.

In my search for better approaches, I came across one of the best attempts to lay out alternative Christian views in a short but profound essay by author and mother Anne Eggebroten. Provoked by serious regret over misguided attempts to discipline her children in true Dobson style, Eggebroten reasons that Christianity does not see sin as some disease in children that adults must control. Rather, in true Augustinian style, sin applies to both parents and children, with graver consequences for adults. Nor is it true that children not taught to submit to parents will not surrender to Christ. God is not an authoritarian judge who must be obeyed. Ample biblical support exists for a God who works more through persuasion, influence, intervention, and conversation than through unyielding power, assertion, and punishment. Ultimately, a child's yielding to God's authority comes not through any good works of the parents but only through God's grace. Instead of worrying that sparing the rod spoils the child, adults should follow the most commonly memorized Twenty-Third Psalm ("The Lord is my shepherd. . . . your rod and your staff—they comfort me"), as Eggebroten insightfully points out. Here the rod comforts rather than spanks. A shepherd carries it to guide, not to beat, the sheep.

One of the most popular secular approaches to parenting gets this Christian view right. Parental Effectiveness Training (PET), a highly successful program that began approximately forty years ago through the leadership of psychologist Thomas Gordon, attempts to strike a vital middle ground between authoritarianism and permissiveness, coaching a kind of parental authoritative yet democratic style. Even though Christianity never enters the picture explicitly, PET understands discipline in terms not unlike those discovered in the Christian tradition. The method requires a rather basic change in attitude toward children similar to what I have called for in reclaiming the vulnerable and yet capable, innocent and yet fallible knowing children of today. Parents should not dogmatically rule over them. Nor should children see the world as owing them everything and their owing nothing in return. Parents are urged to place age-appropriate expectations and responsibility upon them, encouraging a gradual shift from parental direction to children's ownership of problems and internal self-control. Inevitable conflict between parents and children is best solved in a no-lose resolution arrived at through mutual negotiation built around common psychological techniques of nonevaluative listening and honest communication of feelings.

In PET's view, *"parents lose influence by using power and will have more influence on their children by giving up*

Children as Sinful

their power or refusing to use it," in Gordon's emphatic words. Here, Eggebroten has stumbled upon a paradoxical understanding of power that corresponds closely, I believe, with gospel understandings of leadership. Forcing a child to comply with a parental demand to wear a coat, for example, may achieve the immediate goal but in the long run sows seeds of resentment, hatred, noncompliance, and even imitative use of force. Not completely by coincidence, Jesus' sayings suggesting a similar reversal of power—that the first "must be last of all" or the greatest is the "least among you all"—come in close proximity to those gospel passages where Jesus welcomes children.

In a meditation on the prayer of confession in Psalm 51, Anglican priest Samuel Wells reminds us of an insight that surfaced in the last chapter: those without power and freedom are more often sinned against than they are sinners themselves. But Wells adds an additional insight that captures the message of this chapter: "One needs a little power before one can recognize one's true identity: a sinner who can be forgiven, rather than a victim who can protest." His initial words echo the worries of those who have accused Christianity of abuse, but he encourages them and us to take one further step in our spiritual consideration. Only with the freedom to make mistakes are there fewer people to blame. Although Wells does not say so, all this is particularly true for children. Children are more often sinned against than sinners themselves. They need a gradual transfer of power and freedom. The deeper identity of sinner gives children more power than that of victim. With increased knowledge, authority, and control comes growing responsibility and culpability, and—ideally in the Christian story—liberation and grace. Parents do well to keep this trajectory of moral and spiritual development in mind in their parenting.

Recognition of sin goes hand in hand with awareness of grace; as Wells remarks, "Discovering one's ability to sin is a necessary prelude to liberation." Starting with sin, as we have in this chapter, does not mean that sin is the defining characteristic of the human condition. Theologically, the central category is divine redemption, grace, and gift, a topic that the next chapter picks up. But experientially and spiritually, with awareness of sin comes receptivity to grace—perhaps the most obvious answer to the question of why we should talk about sin at all.

Chapter 4

CHRISTIAN FAITH

Children as Gift

———

S in is neither the first nor the last Christian word on children. There is a more basic conception: children as gift. In today's world, politicians and public intellectuals toss this phrase around lightly as a popular cliché, with little awareness of its particular location and specificity within Jewish and Christian covenant traditions. Certainly, other religious and secular traditions have esteemed children. Moreover, people can give public assent to this conviction without needing to confess either Christianity or Judaism. However, its potential for radically challenging distorted contemporary views of children comes only with greater understanding of its distinctive religious roots. In fact, if people knew what it really means in Christian terms to call a child a gift, they might hesitate to do so readily and blithely.

Before turning to the important question of the radical meaning of this Christian claim, as it appears most dramatically in scriptural traditions in which Jesus welcomes children, let us ask: What are some of the distortions of this view of the child as gift? What has led to its demise? The depreciation of its meaning can be partly traced to two developments: the dominating role of other early scriptural traditions and the influence of modernity. The idea was initially eclipsed by the message of other prominent New Testament scriptures in which children are seen as subordinate and necessarily obedient to parents. More recently, the dominating logic and language of a market-driven world makes the subject of gift itself implausible, if not impossible.

THE ECLIPSE OF CHILDREN AS GIFT IN THE PASTORAL LETTERS

As we will see, where the gospel narrative challenges the usual norms of social status and demands stunning respect for children, the Epistles and Pastoral Letters (and the "household codes" in particular) reassert conventional patriarchal family structures. In fact, as some scholars argue, these texts verify that early Christian movements were indeed disruptive to accepted family mores, so much so that these codes must attempt to rebuild hierarchical patterns of household authority.

Household codes is a term applied to such scriptural passages as Ephesians 5:22–6:9 and Colossians 3:18–4:1, which seek to order family relationships among early Christian converts along the lines of similar codes in Greco-Roman and Jewish society ("Wives, be subject to your husbands. . . . Husbands, love your wives. . . . Children, obey your parents. . . . Fathers, do not provoke your children to anger. . . . Slaves, obey your earthly masters. . . . Masters, treat your slaves justly and fairly"). Typically, family members are exhorted to certain behavior in relation to one another—more specifically, subordinates (wives, slaves, children) in obedience to their superiors (husbands, masters, fathers). Children are called to submission, harking back to the Fifth Commandment to honor one's parents. Ephesians and Colossians are commonly attributed to Paul. But most biblical scholars agree that differences in language, style, and theology indicate his followers wrote them after his death, possibly reasserting male authority out of concern about Christianity's fledgling acceptability.

Many people have criticized the household codes as a compromise of Jesus' radical ethic, but few have done so with specific regard to children. The criticism has almost always focused on adult relationships—husband and wife and master and slave—and seldom on parent and child. Feminist theologians, for example, have seen the imperatives about submission as problematic for women. African American theologians have identified problems for those whose heritage includes enslavement. Few people extend the analysis to children.

What would an evaluation of these texts look like if children were themselves counted as primary subjects and, as Jesus sees them, disciples *par excellence*? The argument that Christians significantly modified traditional

Children as Gift

codes on husband-wife and master-slave relationships can be applied to the statements on parents and children. Intriguing differences between Christian household codes and other similar Aristotelian codes indicate that Jesus' affirmation of children's worth was not completely lost. Ephesians and Colossians address both parties and indeed acknowledge the subordinate subject first. By contrast, Aristotelian codes do not speak to the submissive partner at all but only address the more powerful person in each pair, telling the male head-of-household how to administrate proper relations between family members.

That children themselves are spoken to directly as active, rather than passive, agents might not appear in the least unusual today. But it is striking for its time. Christian understanding of the equal value of all life surfaces here, "in a gentle way," as one biblical commentary says. This same commentary calls the leading imperative in Ephesians 5:21—to submit to one another in Christ—a "rather stunning egalitarian principle" with which to frame the code as a whole. It presumably levels all parties, fathers included. Hypothetically, the father should submit to children as children to him. This is perhaps embodied in the request that the father not provoke the child to anger (6:4a). The petition in Colossians 3:21 that fathers not cause children to lose heart is also unique and amends the Fifth Commandment by asking fathers to honor their children.

This final entreaty is an especially tall order. Few parents are without a painful memory of a moment in which they have invariably watched their words of reprimand harm and harden rather than embolden their children's hearts. The imperative to avoid provoking anger and loss of heart is a strikingly relevant guide for parental discipline.

One final Christian ideal tempers these codes. Where Greco-Roman texts give the father ultimate authority, in the Letters obedience belongs to God. This view inevitably modifies ancient ideas of ownership—that parents own children—and unsettles parental authoritarianism. It leaves a loophole for disobedience, even if this loophole has not always been respected over the course of history. As with similar passages on the wife-husband and slave-master relationships, we have here what might be called benevolent patriarchy, a partial advance for Christian love but also a partial demise of the ultimate role that children serve in the synoptic Gospels. These codes qualify parental authority over children while still leaving its dominating and destructive potential intact.

When the final count is in, therefore, these codes come up short. In response to the social and political pressures of the surrounding society, they reverse the more inclusive and socially subversive message of the early Christian community that accorded children new status precisely from their place of insignificance. They reinstitute the honor accorded the adult as ruler and owner of his household, and they diminish the honor granted children as participants in God's reign. The real problem is this: Christian sanction for male authority in these passages has overshadowed the demand to receive children

Children as Gift

as gifts, possibly to children's detriment. Regardless of the initial intention of these codes, from at least the Reformation to the last century they have been used to give supernatural sanction to male power. When ideals of obedience and submission have been wrongly used to control, punish, or harm children, they go against the more fundamental inclination of the early Christian movement to put children as divine gift emphatically at its heart.

THE MARKET-DRIVEN ECLIPSE OF CHILDREN AS GIFT

The problem today is not simply limited readings of the scriptural tradition, however. The problem, as we have already seen in earlier chapters, also results from the powerful controlling logic of market utility that has invaded domestic and social life. People rather unwittingly transfer understandings from the world of production—to compete, win, and be first—to the world of child rearing. This market logic measures everything in terms of costs and benefits to oneself. Every action, judgment, and decision, including those surrounding children's daily lives, is based on commodity exchange for the purpose of promoting one's own interests and the interests of one's own children.

Such a dominating worldview especially disturbs the understanding of children as gift. In fact, principles of market exchange rule out the very premise of gift. In such a world, children are not gifts. They become instead artifacts to be produced, owned, managed, cultivated, and invested. The view of children as product is especially disturbing because it transforms them without remainder into a means to another end.

In a narcissistically hungry society in which parents increasingly look to children to prove their own worth, a child repeatedly becomes a mere extension of adult needs—what one of my colleagues calls the "idolatry of children"—in a whole host of places, not just those identified by Miller, Kohut, and others in Chapter Two. Today adults organize, structure, referee, judge, and cheer for their kids in a huge array of activities—baseball, basketball, and football of course, but also soccer, karate, gymnastics, dance, music, chess, math and mind competitions, local and national spelling bees, and great-book programs. Genuine interest in one's own child is good. But much of the time parents are tempted to cross a fine line between interest and self-centered preoccupation.

This is not simply a matter of inappropriately living one's dreams through one's child. Parents are hypervigilant about their child's success not merely for the sake of the child but for their own self-affirmation, as a sort of proof of their own value. Additionally, this hypervigilance focuses almost exclusively upon one's own offspring and is seldom extended to other children. In fact, other children actually become competitors for limited goods. Finally, as suggested in Chapter One, obsession with such success is not unrelated to the neglect of children with fewer resources in the United States and around the world. Although some people lack the economic and social means to attend to their children's pressing needs, those with greater assets are literally obsessed with their own individual children.

The use of children does not stop with parents and extracurricular schedules. With the spread of the instrumental, consumerist thinking of market capitalism, children are seen as products, consumers, and ultimately burdens in many, many spheres besides the home. Child care manuals, reproductive technology, and most recently human genome research have abetted the transformation of the child from a participant and contributor in the family and society to being a product. New reproductive technologies, whose primary motivation is often to turn a profit, take advantage of prospective parents' vulnerability and encourage the view of child bearing as analogous to making any other purchase in which one selects the most desirable features.

In turn, the U.S. corporate world sees children as a retailer's dream, the next big outlet for a range of products. It has even coined the term *tweens* for the new group of consumers between ages eight and fourteen that constitutes a new $130 billion market. Businesses have created an entire consumptive world of fads and products around children, driven largely by television advertising, where shows are coupled with products or the program itself is the commercial. They want the business, not the well-being, of the twenty-seven million spenders of close to $14 billion a year. Similarly, Hollywood producers make television series that they do not even allow their own children to watch, even though they export them into homes worldwide for profit. Politicians and public intellectuals, in like manner, use children to advance their own reputation and to shape issues as wide ranging as advocating heterosexual marriage to claiming a superior political system. One of the most poignant examples of the use of a child for political gain in recent years was the skirmish over the custody of Elian Gonzalez, a Cuban boy who survived the sinking of a refugee boat when his family attempted to migrate from Cuba to Miami in November 1999. Almost everyone caught up in the fracas had serious trouble genuinely keeping Elian's own good in mind.

It is the third aspect, however—child as burden— that reflects most acutely the final unfolding of capitalism's logic. The market world has no patience for the unproductive, unsettled nature of childhood. In a two-tiered world that separates those who can produce and consume from those who cannot, children, especially poor children, have a stark disadvantage. In such a world, as Todd Whitmore puts it, "no one has intrinsic worth," least of all children; "when persons are neither commodities nor consumers, they are nonentities." Only a residual sense of a child's integrity keeps people from explicitly condoning activities still considered off limits, such as child military service, child prostitution, and child labor. These three uses of children as a means to other ends— war, sex, and work—epitomize the horrendous and extreme outcome of viewing children as products,

Children as Gift

consumers, and in the end nonentities. Covertly, acceptance of a market mentality allows the horrors of such misuse to persist around the world. A genuine Christian view of children as gift radically challenges social and economic complicity in such travesty.

Christianity does not stand innocent in all this. Evidence of the truncation of the idea of children as gift appears in many places. But it also touched the Christian tradition at the very onset of modernity. An intriguing example is in a popular work by the "father of modern theology," Friedrich Schleiermacher, a figure who is also amazingly prophetic and insightful in his deep Christian regard for children. In one of his early reflections, *Christmas Eve: Dialogue on the Incarnation,* a novella about a Christmas celebration in a bourgeois Prussian home, he gives even greater range than his predecessors to the idea of children as God's emissaries. They are portrayed as an instance of "pure revelation" reflecting God's "great gift," which, as embodied by Christmas, is the gift of the Christ child.

Yet, from the beginning of the tale, the Christmas festival reflects the modern encroachment of material presents, in which the exchange of gifts—jewelry, luggage, and books—deceptively promises "progress and happy times ahead." These gifts are meant as tokens pointing beyond themselves to far greater Christian values, but the step from the trappings of Christmas to entrapment in market-driven gift exchange is not as far as Schleiermacher might have hoped or imagined. When gift giving no longer assumes the kind of close, caring attention and gratuitous pleasure described in *Christmas Eve* but instead becomes associated with laborious purchases and accumulation of excessive goods, then comparing children with gifts becomes a potentially unhelpful, even harmful, concept.

Schleiermacher has trouble resisting the idealization of children characteristic of his surrounding culture, which we observed in Chapter One. In *Christmas Eve,* children represent much of what is lost and what many people long for in an increasingly industrialized, market-driven world. They are described as simple, pure, tender, spontaneously joyful and loving, and without anxiety about past or future. In a society that has begun to privatize and separate women, children, emotions, and religion from a public business world where gift giving no longer makes any sense, it is not surprising to find people enamored by and drawn to children's seemingly natural and immediate access to a rich emotional life. Here the Christian idea of children as gift loses its original rich dialectic between gift and the need to care for the gift. The qualities of earnestness, purity, and harmony do not impel adults to children's care in quite the same way that depiction of children's giftedness does in the gospel narratives of Jesus' action, as we will see in a moment. Instead, children represent something for which adults nostalgically yearn.

Even if Schleiermacher could not avoid the impact of modernity, he also anticipated its problems. In his comments on the household codes, he explores with amazingly perceptive insight how parents can injure children:

by failing to honor their concerns; by not responding to their emotions with understanding or control over parental feelings; and, perhaps most telling for today, by living dreams and aspirations through them. He emphasized children's blessings and equal place. Commenting on Schleiermacher's contemporary relevance, church historian Dawn DeVries writes, "In a culture seduced by the totalizing discourse of the market, where children are valued as human capital—as goods to be consumed by the adults in their lives, or as investments whose worth will be measured by future payoff—we can learn from a view that values children as children and that speaks of adults' indebtedness to children." To learn from such a Christian view requires, I believe, not only a rereading of Schleiermacher but a return to the originating scriptures that influenced him to begin with—those passages where Jesus commands his disciples to "let the children come."

Jesus Takes Up Children

Whereas ideas about children being sinful appear primarily in postscriptural debate, the idea of children as gift comes fundamentally from scripture. Even though the New Testament does not make either child rearing or the childhood and family lives of Jesus and his disciples a central topic, it attends to children in other ways. The gospel of Mark has two episodes in which children feature prominently (Mark 9:33–37 and 10:13–16). These accounts also appear in Matthew and Luke in other contexts and with slightly different wording, emphasis, and meaning (Matt. 18:1–5 and 19:13–15; Luke 9:46–48 and 18:15–17). The first episode, in Mark 9:33–37, arises when Jesus catches the disciples in a quintessentially human act: quibbling over who is the greatest. The disciples' fears about their actual and ultimate weakness drive them to vie for first place in the pecking order, pinning their security on being ahead of others. Jesus dramatically inverts this, asserting "whoever wants to be first must be last of all" (v. 35). He takes a child, sets the child in the midst of them, gathers the child into his arms, and says, "Whoever welcomes one such child in my name welcomes me, and whoever welcomes me welcomes not me but the one who sent me." (v. 37).

The second episode in the next chapter, Mark 10:13–16, is provoked by the disciples, who, having learned little from their initial object lesson, try to turn away those who bring children to Jesus. This time Jesus underscores his rebuke with a positive and a negative imperative: let the children come, do not hinder them. Why? For the first time, Jesus directly equates the reign of God with the least of these—with children—as the foundational rationale for receiving them. Let children come, "for it is to such as these that the kingdom of God belongs" (v. 14). In Matthew 19:13–15, the story ends with Jesus laying his hands on them. But in Mark 10:15 Jesus makes a second, more encompassing, and even threatening claim that "whoever does not receive the kingdom of God as a little child will never enter it" (v. 15). Luke's version (18:15–17) further emphasizes the importance of receiving "the kingdom of God as a little child" (v. 17) by

Children as Gift

omitting a final action that appears in Mark, of Jesus taking and blessing the children.

These texts merit a fresh hearing. Until the last decade, people have understood them through the tinted lens of modern romanticized perceptions of children. Scholars and church members alike commonly associate receiving "as a little child" with purity, humility, trust, simplicity, and receptivity. Both Matthew and Luke do refer to "humbling oneself." But the Greek word for *to humble* has itself been read as an emotional and sentimental term, similar to meekness or modesty, rather than as a political and economic term referring to powerlessness or insignificance on a social scale.

Recent scholarship has lifted up the viable error of these modern readings. Mark 10 must be read in light of Mark 9. In other words, the imperative to receive the kingdom "like a child" must be read in light of the imperative to receive children in themselves, in their inferior and vulnerable social status in the first-century world. According to some New Testament authorities, in these passages children represent another instance in which a group—like women, the poor, and the unclean—is marginalized and dominated by more powerful people. They are models of discipleship precisely from this position, as the least in family and society.

On the periphery is exactly where children stood during the early Christian period. Though little is known about their lives, a few general observations can be made. The notion that children might be equal persons in God's sight was foreign to the wider Greco-Roman world. Indeed, they were, in the words of Biblical scholar Judith

LET THE CHILDREN COME

Gundry-Volf, the "least-valued members of society." The free adult male Roman citizen set the standard; children were by comparison deficient, immature, and irrational. As less than fully human, they possessed no legal rights. The *pater,* the male head of the household, had almost absolute control over the fate of those under his authority, especially his progeny. Although parents took pleasure in and expressed affection toward children, unwanted and unruly children did not fare well. Harsh discipline and infanticide through public exposure or abandonment of infants were commonly accepted practices over which fathers had almost complete say. Since male offspring were valued over female, girls were even more susceptible to adult caprice. But for both boys and girls, childhood was brief and subject to the needs and whims of the larger family unit. Children's principle value rested on what they would become, whether a good citizen (if a boy), a wife and mother (if a girl), or a loyal servant (if from the lower class). A family's social and economic survival depended on good use of children—strategic marriage of daughters; transfer of land, trade, and wealth to sons; and passing traditions from generation to generation.

When seen from this perspective, it is hard not to be struck by the distinctiveness of the accounts of Jesus as a public religious teacher indignantly interceding when his followers reprimanded the people for bringing children for his blessing. Equally striking are his claims granting children almost divine status—that in receiving a child one receives Jesus and the one who sent him. These passages starkly invert the assumption that children's religious knowledge depends upon obedience to a divinely ordained paternal authority.

The uniqueness of these claims has roots farther back in Jesus' own Jewish heritage, and it also points forward toward his future place in that lineage. Although Palestinian society was as patriarchal and dependent upon the economic and social functions of children as the surrounding Greco-Roman world, important differences existed. In the Jewish tradition, children were seen as an essential part of God's blessing. This conviction appears most paradigmatically and powerfully in the story of the gift of Isaac to a barren and aging Abraham and Sarah. Isaac ensures God's covenant with Israel. Beginning with Abraham and Sarah's laughter (Gen. 17:17; 18:10–15), powerful scenes of delight over the birth of children are repeated in Hannah's song of thanksgiving at Samuel's birth (1 Sam. 2:1–10) and ultimately in the Magnificat, Mary's echoing prayer of praise of God upon Jesus' conception (Luke 1:46–55). Such is the powerful stream into which Jesus himself steps to be received as God's gift, coming to ensure the people's salvation.

As this implies, the gospel texts on receiving children ultimately have to be placed in their larger context of receiving Christ. Sitting as bookends on both sides of the Mark passages about recognizing children are Jesus' warnings, to his uncomprehending disciples, about his coming death and resurrection (9:30–32; 10:32–34). Mark's Jesus identifies with the vulnerability of the rejected child, subject to the dictates and even betrayal and violence of human struggles for power and security. His gift is ultimately that of the promised Messiah—of death, resurrection, and new life. To welcome a child, then, is to welcome this Christ who so identifies with the child and gives himself as the ultimate gift of love.

In short, these religious traditions put children as a saving gift indelibly at their heart. Most telling in terms of contrasting social practices, Jewish society strictly prohibited exposure and infanticide. Children had a decidedly different status. They not only represented the promise, sign, and guarantee of the covenant; they were also participants in it, to be included in religious observances, educated in the covenant, and routinely brought into and formed by the rich practices and beliefs of love of God and neighbor. The commandment to teach the love of God "to your children and your children's children" steadfastly, diligently—"when you are home and when you are away, when you lie down and when you rise" (Deut. 6:2, 7)—stands at the very heart of Jewish law.

Children in Jewish texts are to receive the content of faith, but in the synoptic Gospels the emphasis is not so much on what is transmitted to them as upon their honorary or gratuitous status. This is a small but important distinction. Nowhere else in Jewish literature, observes Gundry-Volf, are unlearned children, not yet schooled in the knowledge of and obedience to the law, promoted as a model. Children lacked the necessary scriptural wisdom for religious greatness. Such comparison with children would have been considered even more ludicrous in a Greco-Roman context, where children lacked the mental and physical capacities for such status. What stands out in the gospel passages in particular is that children as children qualify as disciples and symbols of the reign of God.

Jesus is not just using children as exemplars, however. He asks his followers to attend to children literally. As important as receiving the kingdom "like a child" is the simultaneous call to receive children in and of themselves. This message is conveyed through what Vernon Robbins labels "demonstrative action." Jesus takes up a child into his arms—a verb that appears only twice in the New Testament in both Mark passages. He blesses and lays his hands on the children. In Luke 9:47, he actually puts the child "alongside" rather than in their "midst," perhaps signaling an even stronger gesture of solidarity. John Dominic Crossan compares these actions of touching, taking, blessing, and laying on of hands to the officially recognized conduct of a father lifting up a newborn to designate its claim for life rather than death. Such a symbolic gesture signified the child's acceptance into the family rather than casting it out.

Gundry-Volf goes further. In these actions, she argues, Mark links Jesus and Christian discipleship to the practices of women. In taking a child up into his arms— a phrase Gundry-Volf finds in other first-century Hellenistic texts specifically connected to women—Jesus imitates a stereotypical female movement, using the low-status activity of women's work as an example for his male disciples and thereby turning social hierarchy completely upside down. He "thus redefines care for children as a mark of greatness."

The many parents who listen to the "Great Judgment" in Matt. 25:31–46 ("For I was hungry and you gave me food . . .") as I have found myself doing, with guilt and self-reproach for not making it out of the home to somewhere else—a prison, hospital, homeless shelter, or food pantry—may take heart. Jesus' message to care for children as among the least and as embodying the one who sent him resembles that of the Great Judgment scene ("Just as you did it to one of the least of these . . . you did it to me," v. 40). Although some contemporary scholars notice this parallel, Martin Luther most boldly proclaimed that parents who properly bear responsibility for children fulfill Matthew 25: "How many good works you have at hand in your own home with your child who needs all such things as these like a hungry, thirsty, naked, poor, imprisoned, sick soul!" This does not excuse parents from wider social commitments, nor permit them to overindulge in their own children. But it does sanction domestic work as one way to participate in bringing God's reign on earth. Ministry begins at home. In fact, Jesus' claim in Mark 9:37 ("Whoever welcomes one such child . . . welcomes me") is an even more proximate and concrete mandate than the generalized religious demand in Matthew 25 to practice hospitality and charity. Those who engage in the social practices of caring for children may, through this very practice, quicken their receptivity to the divine.

RECLAIMING CHILDREN AS GIFT AND TASK

The challenge today is to recapture the "radicalness," as Gundry-Volf expresses it, of the gospel passages in which Jesus welcomes children. This requires change not only in adult attitude but also in children's place within society. In Gundry-Volf's words, "Jesus did not just teach how to make an adult world kinder and more just for children; he taught the arrival of a social world in part defined by and organized around children."

Christian views of children as divine gift challenge and even condemn some contemporary popular views and practices. Children, in essence, inherently question the whole economy of exchange that turns them into a commodity or even a nonentity. If children are gift, wholly unearned, they are ours "only in trust," as Whitmore asserts, coming from and ultimately returning to God. This limits adult power over them and forbids their use as a means to other ends.

Equally important, children are not pure gifts with no strings attached. From the adults around them, children require in return unearned "gifting," without which they will not survive, demanded simply because of what children are in and of themselves. A genuine gift creates an ongoing relationship because a gift leaves a disequilibrium that suggests the hope that sharing gifts will continue *ad infinitum.* Market exchange, by contrast, rigidifies relationships. It aims at an equilibrium in which exchanging money for a product ends the relationship.

Most people who toss around the idea of children as gift know neither the Christian imperatives attached to the claim nor how later Christian history developed them. John Calvin in particular stands out as a sixteenth-century theologian who especially loved the language of children as God's gift and understood the dialectic between gift and task, or the need for a return gifting. This is not so surprising since he saw scripture as a central source of divine truth. If he promotes the theme, it is partly because the Biblical narratives suggest it to him. The idea of children as gift also results from the deep appreciation for divine providence, or God's oversight of human destiny, through which he filters his entire theology. In declaring the fruits of God's purposeful beneficence, he underscores again and again that children are a special blessing.

His commentaries on the stories of barrenness and procreation in Genesis and on references to children in the Psalms are wonderfully illustrative. Speaking about the conception of Isaac, Calvin declares that every birth is like a visit from God. Lifting up the man with many sons who is likened to the happy warrior with a quiver full of arrows in Psalm 127, he repeats a favored phrase of his: the fruit of the womb is God's gift. This phrase, in fact, echoes Elizabeth's greeting of her pregnant kinswoman Mary in Luke 1:42. Calvin departs significantly from other theologians, such as Augustine and Luther, in his reading of the reference in Psalm 8 to "the mouths of babes and infants" singing God's praises. This does not refer allegorically to those young in faith. Rather, for Calvin infants themselves chant God's glory. Here and elsewhere, he identifies children as examples of faith, full participants in the covenant, and "invincible champions of God."

Not unlike the gospel passages, the gift brings its own internal imperative. Precisely when parents recognize children as gifts, they are emboldened to care for

Children as Gift

them properly. In Calvin scholar Barbara Pitkin's words, "this recognition of God's role in child rearing actually inspires and enhances parental care." Calvin's remarks on Psalm 127 confirm this: "Unless men regard their children as the gift of God, they are careless and reluctant in providing for their support, just as on the other hand this knowledge contributes in a very eminent degree to encourage them in bringing up their offspring." Seeing children as God's special favor should temper parental abuse of authority. The demand for obedience, in fact, should be closely coupled with convictions about care of children as gift. Disciplinary problems arise when this is not the case and when obedience is coupled instead with beliefs about a child's depraved nature.

In other words, the gift of children involves paradoxically a corresponding and sometimes costly duty. In New Testament scholar James Bailey's words, Mark's account of Jesus' welcome to children "offers readers the kingdom of God both as gift and task." In the gift of Isaac, God ensures the continuation of God's covenant with Israel but in turn demands Israel's faithfulness. There is a parallel dynamic in the gospel passages. Children as gift demand responsible action on the part of adults, an idea to which we now turn.

Chapter 5

FEMINISM AND FAITH

Children as the Labor of Love

———

This book looks for a more overtly Christian proclamation on children than found in contemporary theology in another unlikely place besides early Christianity and premodern theologians: Christian feminist theology. Retrieving classical Christian views of children as fallible and children as gift can enrich contemporary views. Do Christian feminist theologians have anything distinctive to offer, especially given feminism's checkered history on the family? Haven't feminists simply argued against children as an impediment to women's fulfillment, as many people instantly assume? Moreover, haven't feminists been largely antagonistic toward religion as oppressive? Can anything good about children come out of faith and feminism?

105

My affirmative answer to this last question begins with some background on both secular and religious feminist attitudes toward children, before exploring at greater length two prominent feminist contributions: reclamation of children as the labor of love, and, in the next chapter, as moral and religious agents. Both chapters take earnestly a premise that has implicitly guided the entire book: I ask not only how fresh understanding of children might influence parenthood but also how the contemporary experience of parenting, mothering in particular, shapes understanding of children.

FEMINISTS AND CHILDREN

People hardly associate feminism with advocacy of "family values." Instead, mainstream and conservative folks alike are quite prone to label feminists antichildren, citing as easy proof well-known assertions about liberation in the workplace or random negative remarks about mothering from early inflammatory feminist books. One issue in particular—that of abortion—helped galvanize such perceptions. When considering the subject of children, feminism, and religion, many people conjure up ugly images of the fight over women's right to choose legal abortion surrounding the 1973 *Roe* v. *Wade* decision.

A core premise of second-wave feminism or the feminist politics of the 1960s was indeed women's right to choose against children, whether literally through abortion or more figuratively by forsaking motherhood or choosing to work outside the home. The distinctively radical core of the liberation movement of the 1960s and 1970s was precisely the struggle against subordination of women in the home and at work, especially with regard to reproduction and child care. For most of human history, women's circumstances and survival depended upon their roles in procreation and matrimony. The midtwentieth-century liberation movement insisted instead that women's full personhood should be independent of children, marriage, and motherhood.

This quasi-antichildren stance is a key difference from the first feminist wave that began in the late eighteenth century with Abigail Adams and Mary Wollstonecraft and ended with the achievement of the right to vote in the early twentieth century. Many first-wave feminists fought for the right to speak and act in legal and political spheres. But with few exceptions, they did not essentially challenge the nineteenth-century idealization of women and of mother as the loving, gentle, devoted "angel in the home." Instead, they argued for the value of carrying female domestic virtues of nurture and moral guidance into the public sphere, where men deliberated over pressing social issues such as education and poverty.

By contrast, second-wave feminists disturbed the U.S. public precisely because they disrupted the sanctuary of American home life and contested assumptions at its very heart: male headship and the subordination of women's desires to the needs of children and husband. They proclaimed that the personal was political. That is,

Children as the Labor of Love

the organization of household labor is not merely a private matter. The individual turmoil and personal despair that surfaced in white, middle-class women's consciousness-raising groups across the country had everything to do with the political construction of child rearing as the mother's sole responsibility and with the civic ideal of maternal self-sacrifice. Feminists challenged one particular cultural construction of children: their portrayal as helpless victims of maternal foibles and failures. Such perceptions have destructive political and social ramifications that shape the home—blaming mothers and ignoring fathers—but also extend far beyond the home's private confines.

One powerful spokesperson, Jessie Bernard, saw change in the "future of motherhood" as the most crucial question because it involved such a major restructuring of human relations—women to men, wives to husbands, and, ultimately, parents to children. The goal was, in a word, to "make nonmotherhood as well as motherhood a genuine option . . . to make one as esteemed and acceptable as the other." Women are full persons, not vessels for the delivery of children or appendages to their husbands. Their fulfillment should not be defined wholly around their status as mothers and wives. Nonmothers are not by definition more selfish than mothers are. Women can choose against children for good and worthy reasons.

The fight over reproductive rights therefore embodied two larger, more powerful questions related to children. How will women and men participate in propagating the species? Equally important, what is women's status as human beings in this process? Abortion advocates emphasized not simply women's right to choose but the real cost of raising children once born. Such debate therefore played a symbolic role in the broader struggle over the responsibility of child rearing. Abortion debate represented, in the words of Maura Ryan, "nothing less than a demand for a new social order, one in which women define rather than are defined by their reproductive contribution."

As radical as the claims about reproductive choice was the criticism of the patriarchal family itself. A bumper sticker—actually cited by a critic in an attempt to ridicule those who question the traditional family—blatantly identifies the "family values" that feminists protested: "Unspoken Traditional Family Values: Incest, Alcoholism and Child Abuse." Contrary to the critic's intended gibe, these were real problems nicely blanketed by a society still governed by Victorian ideals. Beneath the surface happiness of suburban, white, middle-class homes of the 1960s, feminists revealed the scandals of depression, addiction, violence, and sexual molestation. They linked these travesties directly to the sexist, patriarchal dynamics of the supposedly harmonious breadwinner-homemaker family.

Not surprisingly, therefore, in discussion about contemporary family crises the women's movement is often one of the most frequently cited factors. Feminism has repeatedly served as a convenient lightning rod for anxiety about family change. Yet popular accusations that feminists destroyed the family or wanted nothing to do with children are grossly overstated. Indeed, a primary motive behind revelations about family violence and abuse has been precisely the protection of children, developed by women who as children themselves were unfortunately not so safely sheltered. Black feminist bell hooks even claims that feminism was the first social movement to draw public attention to how our culture does not love children, commonly seeing them as mere property of parents to do with as they wish. She exaggerates when she says children are a "central" focus of feminism, but she is right to observe a decided interest among feminists in stopping adult violence, in seeing children as individuals, and in rearing them with nonsexist values.

Contrary to the instant conclusion that feminism caused family dissolution, the rigid gender roles of the narrowly construed breadwinner-homemaker family would have come under increasing stress with or without feminist critique. A multitude of forces disrupted families in the twentieth century, among them birth control, modern technology, market capitalism, increased education and democratization, and the movement from an industrial to a service economy. Feminism was as much a reaction to these other developments as a cause.

Feminists were, of course, happy to lend their support. They did seriously disrupt previous assumptions about who cares for children and how. Despite optimistic hopes, they certainly did not find a way to weave children back into the fabric of full and equal adult lives, as critics of feminism have chided. But, for that matter, neither have men or those who oppose feminism. As we observed in Chapter One, children have been the missing factor in modern equations of human happiness across the board.

Feminism's relative silence on how to integrate children into egalitarian families is understandable in such a context. Women seeking liberation readily recognized that they had borne immense costs raising children in a modern society that ultimately fails to value them or support such labor. By necessity, the question of who cares for children if women no longer make the job their complete aim in life was not at the heart of early feminist consideration, whether or not any kind of malicious animosity toward children was intended. However, although children were not the first order of business by any means, neither did most feminists wholly disavow them.

The sheer amount of work and the intense emotional passions of mothering also left little time, space, energy, or even desire to offer up reflections on children for public consumption. Several years ago, when I worked for an institute devoted to research on health, faith, and ethics, I was struck by the number of essays I came across that were written by men offering their personal reflections on the hardships of stillbirth, miscarriage, and other reproductive dilemmas. Where, I wondered, were women's voices? Women are overwhelmed, I realized, with simply living with these complex realities, much less reflecting on them publicly. In other words, both the social structures of child rearing and the cultural assumptions about women's roles have actively discouraged creative passions beyond children, including articulating

Children as the Labor of Love

what women have learned from them or developing any kind of feminist advocacy for them.

Ultimately, however, demonized feminist texts and the high visibility of such hot issues as abortion and women's equal rights overshadowed the many feminist claims about children that have been present from the beginning. Although people tend to paint feminists in monochromatic color, feminists have not uniformly dismissed children, even if some oppose the patriarchal family or are outspoken about the hazards of motherhood. In the past two decades, many factors have changed how feminists regard children.

In particular, fresh views from women of color and second- and third-generation feminists, greater awareness of the influence of class, frustrations in the workplace, and intensified globalization have revealed diverse child-bearing experiences and forced reconsideration of previously uncontested feminist assumptions about women's desires and needs. For those in marginalized communities for whom mere survival is sometimes difficult, mothering, children, and strong families have immense value, men need jobs and education along with women, and "choice" is not the only moral consideration in bearing and rearing children. In contexts of social oppression and even genocide, children and child rearing offer a dramatic means for political resistance. Neither motherhood nor children, then, pose the same kind of hardship that they did for white, middle-class U.S. women of the 1960s. Instead, impediments to freedom and fulfillment include other major problems, such as racism, first-world imperialism and materialism, lack of good jobs and education, and ecological and health crises.

Two decades ago, motherhood at least became a more acceptable topic. This development coincided with a general shift from an early liberal feminism, oriented around obtaining equal rights in the workplace, to a more women-centered feminist approach, oriented around reclaiming values intrinsic to women's distinctive experiences, including pregnancy and childbirth, as a more trenchant critique of male-defined society. This change is most clearly marked by the publication and popularity of three pivotal late-seventies publications: Adrienne Rich's *Of Women Born* (1976), Nancy Chodorow's *The Reproduction of Mothering* (1978), and Sara Ruddick's *Maternal Thinking* (1980). All three books have had an immense impact on understanding mothers, although they did not radically alter the general perception of the women's movement as antagonistic toward families. Nor, for the most part, did they reflect the experiences of women outside the white middle class. More generally, some feminists who stand solidly on the progressive side of the current family debate, such as sociologist Judith Stacey, became alarmed about the potentially detrimental influence on feminist politics of the recent profamily leanings of prominent early feminist leaders, such as Betty Friedan. Will waxing nostalgic about motherhood, children, and home undermine efforts to challenge the ubiquitous subordination of women?

Even in raising this concern Stacey willingly admits the nagging problems left in the wake of the liberal feminist agenda of equality and independence. She concludes an essay that admonishes profamily feminists by acknowledging three personal traumas that have raised legitimate issues: involuntary singlehood, involuntary childlessness, and single parenthood. Behind these ordeals, Stacey identifies three sweeping social concerns that feminists must face. If the conventional nuclear family is failing, what are viable, healthy alternatives beyond toleration of instability and diversity? What is the place of heterosexuality, an institution and practice that has been criticized but not fully appreciated? Finally, the question that feminists have especially neglected and that motivates this book: What do children really need?

Motherhood is still a more acceptable topic than children. Children have yet to receive the same kind of attention. If feminists like Stacey worry that the focus on family subverts radical liberation politics, a focus on children is sure to evoke a similar concern.

Yet feminists can no longer avoid the question of what children really need, even if it means hard choices when the needs of parents and children do directly conflict. Feminism has had a big impact on the contemporary family, not simply among adherents but also among those who do not endorse its claims. It has dramatically changed family dynamics. Women and men, whose parents accepted women's role in the home and believed that women should yield authority to men, are trying to forge relationships of far greater mutuality. Many people are left standing with the challenging problem of how to figure children back into such a family.

A few years ago, when I submitted an essay for a book on mothers, the editors asked me to explain why I referred not only to mothers but also more broadly to families. I argued that a mother is only a mother in relation to children, father, and family. Feminists may simply not realize the extent to which redefining the position and value of mothers requires concurrent redefinition of children's lower status. Although many people study mothers, or for that matter children, as a distinct topic, I am troubled by a sharp and rather artificial separation between the two. How can one genuinely rethink motherhood without rethinking childhood and vice versa? Parenting and children stand in critical relationship to one another.

FEMINIST THEOLOGY AND CHILDREN

Many people will be surprised to hear of yet another difference among feminists: not all feminists reject religion as hopelessly patriarchal. Moreover, by and large Christian feminists have done a better job of putting and keeping children in the conversation than secular feminists.

Addressing the subject of children has been an uphill battle on this front as well. Christian theology itself has tended to lump women and children together as subordinate to and dependent on men. As early as the gospel of Matthew, where the author totals the five thousand men miraculously fed "not counting women and children" (Matt. 14:21), women and children have often been dismissed *en masse.*

Activism on behalf of children stood at cross-purposes with the initial objectives of early feminist theologians. As relative newcomers to the study of religion in the 1960s and 1970s, they were highly aware of their precarious position as "honorary men" in a public world of church and academy theretofore defined by exclusion of women and children. They had plenty of other work to do simply challenging harmful theological doctrines, such as God made in a male image, manhood as the criterion for priesthood, women as the source of sin, and self-sacrifice as the highest ideal of the Christian life.

Feminists in theology supported the wider feminist movement by recognizing the crucial role of religious beliefs in providing ideological support for patriarchy. They disputed religiously endorsed assumptions that men are the divinely ordained head of household and that all women desire—and indeed need—motherhood to become fully human according to their God-given "special nature." Some identified disputing Christian endorsement of the male-dominated family as *the* major key to unraveling patriarchy.

Christian feminist arguments for gender-role equality and shared procreative responsibilities had to contend with powerful connections between the maintenance of strong families and the survival of a religious tradition or ethnic group. This is apparent in particular communities struggling on the margins, such as the Jewish community, African American families, and fundamentalist Christian

LET THE CHILDREN COME

groups. But these communities are not alone. Even the most liberal religious institutions are inherently conserving and conservative. They seek to preserve important traditions. This otherwise valuable aim is all too often confused with a desire to preserve the patriarchal status quo. Religion in general has frequently equated establishment of distinct child-bearing roles in the patriarchal family with a religious faith community's welfare.

Nonetheless, despite many obstacles, feminist theologians have taken a stronger position of advocacy for children than secular feminists have. For the most part, early feminist theologians avoided blaming children for women's plight. Few have been unabashedly antifamily. High regard for children actually began long before secular feminism's turn to motherhood in the 1970s and 1980s and also received new energy from this shift.

Connections to religious traditions acted as a partial restraint. In the early nineteenth and twentieth century, women of faith in a variety of contexts championed children's needs and rights through a proliferation of women's organizations and the founding of community institutions such as orphanages and schools. It was precisely the concern for children that frequently led religious women into public activism. Such concern is still evident, not only in social advocacy for children among churchwomen but also in the feminist theological scholarship of the last decade. Children may impede women's progress in some respects. But if the larger church, religious scholarship, and society as a whole fail to take up children's cause, still seeing it as "women's work,"

Children as the Labor of Love

religious women will continue to work on behalf of children.

Yet there are still problems and limits. First, feminist theologians have worked harder to restructure adult relationships than to take the next step of reconstructing the relationship between parents and children. Few consider questions about obligations between adults and children in an egalitarian family, or about the nature of mutuality when children, who are temporarily dependent and unable to participate fully as equals, enter the picture. What specific concepts should replace previously powerful religious motifs of headship, submission, sacrifice, and obedience? How can ideals of empowerment be extended to children without disregarding women's gains or the need for adult wisdom?

Second, when feminist theologians have thought about children, they often focused more on aberrations in child rearing, such as domestic violence, abuse, sexist gender roles, and poverty, than on constructive suggestions for better parenting. An understandable ambivalence about the hazards of patriarchal Christianity has inhibited efforts to reappropriate valuable contributions. But if the critique of the Christian family is such a major linchpin in challenging patriarchy, why have there been so few serious efforts to reconstruct workable Christian alternatives that factor in children?

Finally, for those feminist theologians who have included children in their work, the subject has still almost always remained secondary to other primary causes. Roughly speaking, constructive efforts to address children

LET THE CHILDREN COME

fall into three groups, closely related to changes in the wider feminist movement. The earliest and most widely recognized theological advocates for social justice, such as Beverly Harrison and Rosemary Radford Ruether, took up children, as early liberal feminists did, out of concern about procreative choice and reproductive responsibility. Children deserve consideration because they suffer from some of the same distortions of human rights and public policies that women have encountered for decades, such as domestic abuse, poverty, and denial of fair representation in decision making. Corresponding to the renewed feminist interest in women's unique maternal knowledge, a second group thought about children as an offshoot of new understandings of God as mother and experiences of pregnancy, childbirth, nursing, and child care. Such maternal encounters spark spiritual growth and even epiphany about divine and human virtues. Most recently, concern about strong families and the health of civil society has provoked a third group to worry about children in terms of the damage done by liberal and libertarian values of individual rights and personal choice.

In general, when compared with other contemporary theological colleagues and secular feminist peers, these three groups of feminist theologians stand up amazingly well. They have given significant attention to children from a range of perspectives. However, this attention is often funneled through other priorities, whether social justice, motherhood, or the common good. In each case, reimagining children and child care has been an important subtext, but it has seldom been the main text.

The task now is to read between the lines for ways to articulate more vigorously the important insights that feminist theology suggests. The strongest position on children must incorporate the strengths of all three groups. That is, with the "social justice feminists" it must affirm the prerequisites of personal and social equity and respect the rich diversity in family life. With the "motherhood feminists," it must honor maternal experience as a source of genuine knowledge about children and religion. Finally, with the "common good feminists," it must counter the problems of severing procreative choice from sexual commitment and social responsibility and recognize the value of strong families for society.

CHILDREN AS WORK

Children require work, and lots of it. Feminists in general have made us well aware of this material reality. They have legitimately demanded that fathers and society bear more of the economic and emotional burden. They have called for a revaluing of such work. In so doing, they challenge the modern idealization of children as entirely malleable and of nurture as something that women innately and easily perform.

Across differences of race, class, and nation, women around the world share one striking commonality: they shoulder an enormous amount of indispensable labor, much of it related to children, with little compensation or recognition. To borrow political scientist Hilda Scott's penetrating words, women's unpaid productive and reproductive work "underpins the world's economy, yet it is peripheral to the world's economy as men define it, and therefore has no value. It is this that makes women a category of persons who are economically invisible, whose work is non-work, who have no experience or skills, who don't need a regular income because their husbands support them."

In a fantastic twist of language, the hard labor of child rearing has been defined as "nonwork." It has seldom been factored into economic and social equations; it is simply presumed. The absurdity of this became apparent as more women moved into the workforce in the last several decades. As they assumed increased economic responsibility without fundamentally redefining their role as the mainspring of family life, they encountered a dilemma already quite familiar to many other working women of the world: what Arlie Hochschild popularized as the "second shift." Based on time-use studies, she estimates that over a year women work an "extra month of twenty-four-hour days." In one study, women employed outside the home "averaged three hours a day on housework while men averaged 17 minutes; women spent fifty minutes a day of time exclusively with their children; men spent twelve minutes." Adding paid work to an already overloaded domestic day suddenly reveals previously undocumented and undervalued work hours.

In some ways, none of this is terribly surprising, even if the figures are startling. Many women have always worked from the crack of dawn until the setting sun. A 1980 United Nations report estimated that women perform two-thirds of the world's labor, receive 10 percent of the pay, and own 1 percent of the property.

What is new is the attempt to reorganize and redefine child-rearing labor and, coinciding with this, the changing view of children. Many secular feminists insist on redefinition of work and children in economic terms. Scott says society needs to elevate "unpaid work to a place in the economy equal to that of paid work" and establish it "as a legitimate economic category" with its own criteria and its own rewards for both women and men. Some feminists even suggest monetary compensation for homemaking through governmental mechanisms, such as splitting the income of the breadwinner or offering tax benefits for children and stay-at-home parents.

Other feminists, sometimes characterized as "gynocentric" or "radical" in their high appraisal of women's experience, focus on political and social redefinition of children and their care. Women gain particular knowledge from birthing, nursing, and nurturing that suggests a more fundamental criticism of dominant male assumptions about power and prestige based on greed, self-promotion, and aggression. In this view, domestic work is not a hindrance to women but a valuable resource that culture and men ignore at their own peril. Men's distance from child care harms them as well as children's development. Inactive fathers cause boys to flee from intimacy and attachment, girls to become enmeshed with their mothers, and both boys and girls to develop misogynist hatred of women, who have little power in the real world and who represent that from which children must separate. In other words, the unequal distribution of child-rearing labor—when only women mother—reproduces male dominance and perpetuates the war between the sexes.

This leads many feminists to argue not just for economic or cultural redefinition of children but for a fairer reorganization of household labor: in essence, more baby care for men. Having children creates a major crisis in negotiating domestic responsibilities equitably. In almost all cases, women slide down the slippery slope from birthing to assuming an ever-growing proportion of child-related tasks. In pragmatic cost-benefit language, the "headstart effect" of biology, pregnancy, attachment, breastfeeding, and initial infant care, on top of socialization about child care as a female job, reduces a woman's "bargaining power" in the marriage and family market and initiates a process that leads to heavier investment in children and home. Nearly all couples therefore need some form of "countertipping." That is, men need more time with children simply to catch up with women's physical labor and attachment.

In all this, whether approached economically, culturally, or strategically, children are in essence seen as labor but now fundamentally redefined. Early liberal feminists simply followed standard modern assumptions about children. Trying to create a life beyond motherhood, they talked about children as if they were something one does on the side, requiring only a small portion

Children as the Labor of Love

of one's adult years. Later feminists corrected this construction, insisting instead that children are in fact arduous work that ought to be more fairly shared.

CHILDREN AS THE LABOR OF LOVE

Have secular feminists adequately understood the nature of this work and the necessary changes for women, men, and children? There are important benefits to these new definitions of children as work, but much is left to be desired from a Christian feminist perspective. Without meaning to sound like a Hallmark card, missing from these deliberations is the idea of commitment, and even love. Children are not just any kind of work. They are a special kind of labor of love, evoking unique obligations, intimacies, and transformations because, unlike any other work, they are subjects in themselves capable of their own work, love, gifts, and contributions.

Why have many secular feminists not grappled with this? I propose it is partly because moral and religious beliefs have been almost entirely bracketed and disregarded as either unimportant or simply destructively patriarchal. Appealing primarily or only to economic and social categories truncates the meaning of children and the responsibilities of parenthood. A fuller understanding of children and children's care requires drawing on richer cultural and religious language.

There has been real reason, of course, to bracket

love. For too long, it was presumed that women did child care completely out of love. But to ignore attachment, affection, and devotion reduces care of children to merely one more economic and political task. Not only do we need to rethink work, therefore; we also need to rethink love. On this score, Christian feminists have agreed heartily with the general premise that domestic work must be shared more equitably. But they have also directed considerable energy to challenging traditional Christian ideals of love.

Sacrificial Love for Children

Many feminists hope to undermine governing views of the mother in Western society as eternally bountiful, forever giving, and always self-sacrificing. But few realize the extent to which they must wrestle with Christianity to do so. Christianity has remained a steadfast factor in institutionalizing unconditional maternal love. Congregations have long upheld sacrifice as the ideal after which good Christians should strive. Women and mothers have especially taken this understanding to heart.

An initial challenge to commonly accepted views of sin and love arose when Valerie Saiving declared self-diminishment rather than self-aggrandizement the most common temptation for women who birth and care for children. This in turn led her to question doctrines of love as complete self-giving constructed in response to male views of sin as pride and self-conceit. Since then, many others have taken the next logical step and argued that

Christian love should involve not self-sacrifice but a more radical mutuality or equal give-and-take. Unconditional sacrifice, often equated with love as *agape,* is not the highest Christian ideal. *Caritas,* a mutuality or equal regard that includes but does not idealize sacrifice, is more fundamental to the Christian message.

In all the discussion about mutuality's superiority, however, few people have given much thought to children. This is a serious oversight because it is precisely children's presence that makes just love between spouses and partners especially difficult. Those involved in mutuality are not always like-minded adults but women, men, and children in various stages of development and relationship. They are not the static, independent, or mature people often presumed by theological and philosophical discussion but rather children who have needs and cannot fully reciprocate, and adults who in their care for children need the support of others.

Roman Catholic ethicist Christine Gudorf stands alone in her 1985 attempt to understand the nature of Christian love explicitly in relationship to children. Most children do not need, she asserts, the kind of unconditional love that Christianity has upheld as the ideal and that adults, with the help of psychology, have projected on mothers. She came to this conclusion partly out of her being disturbed by the almost universal perception of her and her husband's adoption of two medically handicapped children as exemplary of heroic, self-sacrificing Christian love. She found this a "very faulty" interpretation resulting not just from a gross misunderstanding of

LET THE CHILDREN COME

parenting but also from a distortion of the ethic of love upheld by Jesus.

Although initially she and her husband gave considerably of themselves, Gudorf contends that this giving was never unconditional or self-disregarding. It involved a necessary self-interest that actually enhanced their capacity to give. As parents, they realized that their strenuous efforts to provide for their children rebounded to their credit, and that, inversely, failing to do so would have discredited them. In a word, from the beginning loving care for their children involved the hope and the expectation that the "giving would become more mutual."

As such parental honesty reveals, the theological dynamics of love are more complicated than most Christian theology has presupposed. Love, particularly the love between parent and child, involves ample self-giving certainly, but self-giving must never become the ideal. As Gudorf proclaims, love involves sacrifice, but it "aims at mutuality." Moments of self-diminishment, even the moment of sacrifice on the cross, are, in her words, "just that—moments in a process designed to end in mutual love." The cross is not a good in itself or a sacrifice to be imitated. Jesus' suffering came as a consequence of his radical efforts to create just and loving communities and aimed at bringing people into such relationship with others and God. Nor were the sacrifices that Jesus urged disinterested. When he asked people to face persecution, give up their possessions and family, and follow him, these remained means to a more important end. He consistently held out the promise of a greater prize of rich return in

God's kingdom known even now in the small moments of love returned within this life.

An exaggerated ideal of sacrifice, then, should not be hung over the heads of parents struggling to love their children. It denies parents the complexity of parental labor—that vesting one person with full responsibility for parenting may not be wise or even possible, that parents may love their children but cannot and should not sacrifice everything for them, and that some of the labor of love is just that—labor without much immediate love but in need of the promise of relief and returned love over the long haul. An exaggerated ideal of sacrifice harms people, particularly women, who are already overprogrammed to give endlessly, leaving them ashamed of the self-interest that naturally accompanies their labor. So the mother who says "I'm a better mother because I work outside the home" is not trying to deny children's value or to dismiss the problems that working and mothering creates. Instead she is trying to name the delicate interplay between love of others and self-love that, under optimal circumstances, ought to flourish in the work and love of children.

Mutual Love with Children

What does mutual love look like when the participants are children? This moves into even less previously charted territory. Children's love can be effusive and spontaneous, but they are also in no position initially to offer love in the same way as adults. Physically and cognitively, until a certain age children are not capable of the kind of inverse thinking and acting required for genuine mutuality in which one can think and feel oneself into the other's skin. Nor are they prepared or able to meet the responsibilities of care or offer material aid to others. As we saw in Chapter Three, many classical Christian theologians recognized that children should not be held as morally responsible or culpable as adults, who have far greater means and opportunity to perfect their ability to do good or evil. What more does feminist theology say?

Unfortunately, feminist theologians are just as guilty as many others in their indiscriminate use of the term *mutuality*. In discussions of just love in general, it is amazing how seldom children are mentioned. I became acutely aware of this, and found myself increasingly troubled about what I have come to call "sloppy mutuality," while reading Carter Heyward's highly controversial book, *When Boundaries Betray Us*. Drawing on her traumatic experiences in counseling, Heyward argues that traditional therapy establishes a destructive hierarchy of power between client and therapist that makes genuine healing impossible. The rigid boundaries and lack of mutuality, with therapist as expert and client as dependent, ultimately betrays and abuses clients. Genuine love, she says, should not rule out mutuality "*anywhere* in our lives," including in therapy.

Most of the controversy sparked by her book centered on the question of appropriate professional boundaries. Though certainly important, this seriously sidestepped a more troubling issue: sloppy understanding of mutuality. Many people banter around the term, but it is not entirely clear that everyone is talking about the

Children as the Labor of Love

same thing or even using the term in the same way all the time. Some use the term to talk about sexual intimacy; those who understood the term in this way worried that Heyward opened the door to sexual impropriety on the part of the clinician. Others mean equal regard. Still others mean shared power and responsibility. Does mutuality mean mutual intimacy, equal power and agency, or shared responsibility? Or is it more accurate to say that it means all of these ideas in different times and places?

Heyward is not alone, then, in her ill-defined use of mutuality. Her book simply provides a needed impetus to move toward an understanding more inclusive of children, parents, and other relationships of temporary inequality. The need to qualify the claim that love is only genuine when it is completely and fully mutual becomes most apparent when the participants include children.

Hierarchy has become a bad word; it is often narrowly equated with authoritarianism and sometimes with patriarchy. Yet hierarchy is not bad in and of itself. The conflict surrounding Heyward's book makes clear that we need to recognize the reality of "transitional hierarchy," a temporary inequity between persons—whether of power, authority, expertise, responsibility, or maturity—that is moving toward but has not yet arrived at genuine mutuality. Power-over relationships are thus not destructive by definition; they are harmful when they are unchanging and exploitative. In other words, the measure of mutuality is partly determined by where it is moving and its intentions. Most advocates of mutuality fail to note that it cannot be applied across the board to all relationships

LET THE CHILDREN COME

without qualification. Consideration of children forces us to recognize that conceptions of mutuality are multivalent or age-, expertise-, and context-dependent.

It is significant that Gudorf describes the kind of love she is talking about with children as a "process" that "seldom begins mutually." In *From Culture Wars to Common Ground,* my colleagues and I agree. We reiterate that Christian love as mutuality inevitably "means different things for different family members at different points in family and individual life cycles." In a transitional hierarchy, the adult has more authority and (hopefully) life-earned wisdom and maturity, and the child must be allowed greater latitude in self-indulgence. Developmentally, children and youths need to experiment with a range of roles and desires. They need a certain protected sphere of irresponsibility that allows them to play with words, actions, and commitments for which they do not yet have to answer. Self-assertion, self-aggrandizement, and outright selfishness are necessary as part of the gradual evolution toward a life that brings together self-fulfillment and self-giving as critical interrelated components of Christian love. Although parents must make difficult, discerning choices about when to indulge and when to override children's desires, for the most part this discrepancy between adults and children warrants gracious leniency on the part of adults toward children's neediness.

New parents in turn enter a period of "transitional renunciation." Just as we questioned distorted ideals of Christian sacrifice, we also need to question what pastoral theologian Brita Gill-Austern describes as the

Children as the Labor of Love

"increasingly wide-spread tendency to condemn all forms of self-giving." As she asserts, "Christian self-sacrifice is not pernicious by definition." Caring for children requires turning down the avenues of personal gratification and individual fulfillment that abound outside the family. Especially during a child's first few years, parents must restrict their own desire in order to meet a vulnerable child's more acute need.

Here, a key question becomes how to distinguish life-giving sacrifice from life-denying. Toward the conclusion of her essay, Gudorf offers one standard: "An act is only a loving act if it has the potential to provoke loving response, however far in the future. Acts of no matter how much self-sacrifice, which support or encourage unloving actions or attitudes, are not acts of love." Theological ethicist Barbara Andolsen proposes more concrete criteria. Although she does not apply these guidelines to the parent-child relationship, they certainly pertain. There is place for sacrifice, she argues, when practiced by the privileged on behalf of the oppressed, when a party in greater need has a *prima facie* claim on others, and when occasions of sacrifice can be balanced out over the long run. On all three scores, adults often owe children sacrificial love, recognizing their often subordinate position, accepting the mandate that children *qua* children place upon adults, and awaiting a time when most children will, in turn, give back to family and community what has been generously bequeathed to them.

As this final clause indicates, parents also owe children full comprehension of the expectations that await them. U.S. society as a rule demands too little of children. I remember my surprise years ago when I discovered the extensive household duties—shopping, cooking, cleaning, and so forth—expected of the children of two Filipino families in a congregation I served while doing graduate work. These children performed tasks that I had almost come to assume children as children were incapable of doing. In the fallout of modern notions, U.S. society largely views children as too delicate, too incompetent, or too busy to contribute.

In *Also a Mother,* I countered this presupposition by arguing for what I called the "pitch-in" family. Embodied in this pithy phrase is the idea that, given love, children also need daily exercise of the practice of giving to others, first respecting their siblings and parents and contributing around the house and eventually participating in the betterment of the wider community. Quite honestly, this idea has actually been harder to implement than I first supposed. Asking more of my children than is dictated by social mores or requested by their peers' parents has not been easy, even when I recognize that the complaint "None of my other friends have to do this" is often just a convenient excuse for evading responsibility. Yet, even if it meets with far greater resistance, the narrative of the pitch-in family is more appropriate to the knowing children of today than the cookies-and-milk narrative in which an ever-ready mother always provides.

Ultimately, although more needs to be said about responsibility for and of children within the wider community—a topic to which the next chapter turns—any

Children as the Labor of Love

attempt to redefine children as the labor of love from a Christian perspective is unfinished until it considers love's limits and impossibilities. Popular rhetoric about mutuality can easily mislead people into misunderstanding the complicated nitty-gritty realities of daily family life. Mutuality over the long haul means inevitable and repeated failure and injury. Inherent limitations—of time, energy, understanding, and fatigue—as well as factors that religious types would simply call "sin"—selfishness, anxiety, misunderstanding, and hostility—impede its implementation.

Consequently, reckoning with the harsh actualities and occasional impossibilities of implementing mutuality in love's labor requires clearing a way for forgiveness and the grace of reconciliation, whether this comes through formal Christian rituals of religious confession or through nonconfessional, nonreligious means of deliberate, respectful conversation. However understood, achieving genuine mutuality in relationship to children and in the care of children is not finally a matter of economics, social perception, will, or personal resolution but a matter of grace that we welcome when it happens. "In final analysis," as pastoral theologian Herbert Anderson says so well in his inimitable Lutheran style, "justice in marriage is not something we achieve. It is something we discover. . . . For those who follow Christ . . . it is something that is given rather than earned. For Christian persons in marriage, it is impossible [therefore] to separate justice from gratitude."

We talk about this in *From Culture Wars to Common Ground* by naming mutuality as a "strenuous ethic." We also give a rather long list of crucial requirements, which might be expanded to identify children explicitly. Seeing children as the labor of love requires strenuous practice of respect for the selfhood and dignity of the other, taken as seriously as one expects the other to regard one's own selfhood. This means pursuing the welfare of the other as vigorously as one pursues one's own. Such mutuality or equal regard does not appear overnight but evolves as people change and develop in their relationships. It requires a complex process of intentional conversation and deliberation about its concrete enactment in the lives of those involved. Finally, its achievement is not fully within human power but always occurs within the realm of the common good and, from a Christian perspective, within the realm of God's influence.

Chapter 6

FEMINISM AND FAITH

Children as Agents

To view children as work, even as valuable work, entails a serious problem to which the last chapter pointed and the entire book alludes. It threatens to reduce them to nothing more than one more job to be argued over, divided up fairly, and then done, whether by mothers, fathers, or the wider community. In today's popular language, children simply become a social resource for changing men or human social capital for sustaining democracy. These ultimately inadequate views are deficient precisely because they tempt us to lose sight of a more essential conviction: children as ends in themselves. It makes sense to claim that child rearing deserves greater respect and is something fathers should share, but it is risky to do so without proclaiming children's inherent value regardless of what they demand or produce. Neither the child nor the parent is a means to another end—neither the mother as servant to the child, as feminism has powerfully asserted, or the child as servant to the parents, as feminist theology presupposes, which I will argue in a moment. Only when this basic claim is asserted are adults truly free and empowered to serve children and children genuinely liberated to serve society.

The idea of children as actors in their own right is not new, but feminist theology gives it renewed meaning. Although some secular spokespersons are discovering the notion as if anew, feminist theologians have assumed it for a long time. They have talked about it primarily in terms of children's agency. Two aspects of children as agents receive particular attention. First, feminist theology upholds children as persons created in God's image and therefore deserving of basic human rights accorded all people of any age, color, or creed. Second, it celebrates children as a source of spiritual insight. In my threefold characterization of feminist theology, the social-justice feminists and common-good feminists have especially promoted the view of children as moral agents in terms of their intrinsic physical, material, emotional, and political entitlements. The motherhood group has advanced the idea of children as spiritual agents in terms of children as God's representatives with the potential for significant impact upon adults. All three groups demonstrate how religious convictions about human creation and divine desire can lend support to an ideal of children as agents that is worthy of wider public affirmation beyond the particularity of a Christian perspective.

Recently, a growing interest in children's spirituality has emerged. A great deal more needs to be said about this and about children's developing moral capacities. Here I make some initial observations about children's spirituality and morality. I then turn, however, to the equally intriguing question of what is demanded from adults morally and spiritually in relationship to children as moral and spiritual agents. As in the rest of the book, my focus is not so much on the important question of *how children think* about the good and the right or about God. I remain interested for now in figuring out *how adults think about children* as moral and spiritual agents.

CHILDREN AS MORAL AGENTS

U.S. society has long pronounced the family a haven of love and affection. Feminist theologians insist that it must also be a beacon of justice. They primarily have had women's situation in mind, but the principle also applies to children. Social-justice and common-good feminists have promoted the welfare of children by addressing a range of social, economic, and political injustices, including child abuse, disdain for the "bodyright" of children, poverty, and child-unfriendly public policies and legislation. In each case, an enhanced view of children as moral agents challenges mistreatment of children as object rather than subject in their own right. The theological bottom line is this: as created in God's image, children merit the immense respect and empathy all too often unjustly and wrongly denied them.

Some feminists in the justice group, such as religion scholar Paula Cooey and pastoral theologian Pamela Couture, fight for children threatened by the hardships of impoverishment. The Children's Defense Fund says one in six children in the United States continue to live in poverty and are more likely to be poor today than twenty or thirty years ago. But material poverty is not the only problem, in Couture's opinion. Children also suffer from the poverty of insubstantial connections with families, neighborhoods, and supportive social institutions. Christians have a special responsibility to promote children's resilience, expanding pastoral care of the individual to community action. In fact, churches and theological schools "are poor," she declares, "to the extent that they are tenuously connected" to children.

Feminist theologians such as Couture and Cooey also insist that the international public has an important role. They stand behind the United Nations Convention on the Rights of the Child, developed over a ten-year period and adopted in 1989 (with the United States one of two countries that have not ratified it). The treaty strives to put into place common understanding about what children need in order to flourish: education, a caring family, protection from exploitation and abuse, and a voice on significant issues. Couture names children's rights as a key normative international framework for unified advocacy.

The intent is not to assert the rights of children over those of parents, or to dismiss the importance of two-parent households. These are fears largely harbored by conservative Christians who lobby hard for preserving parents' exclusive rights over their children's lives. Rather, feminist theology invites a deeper discussion of the rights and responsibilities of both children and parents.

Others have focused on bodily rights. Although Western society has promoted political and economic rights, it has been slow to shed its assumptions of male ownership of women and children's bodies. Infringement of bodily rights, most apparent in long-term child sexual abuse, seriously impedes moral agency by diminishing the capacity for intimacy and empathy—capacities essential for moral action. Instead, abuse generates feelings of powerlessness, paralysis, mistrust, and inadequacy. Bodily integrity is therefore an absolute "prerequisite for full personhood and moral agency," as Christine Gudorf remarks, and needs to be a central component of Christian sexual ethics in relationship to children. She champions children's bodyright, or the right to control one's body, as fundamental to moral agency, as a key means to empower them to resist abuse, and as a morally appropriate mandate in itself. Recognition of bodyright means that the child's wishes "should be solicited, heard, and considered in any decision about the child's bodyself."

Children's bodyright is inadequately supported by theology and often overlooked by the very adults presumed to care most intimately for children. This has been dramatically revealed in the failure to take children

Children as Agents

seriously in recent child sexual abuse scandals in the Catholic church, not only by the sexual offenders themselves but also by others in the church. An all-male Catholic hierarchy, often far removed from children and their care, failed to see children's bodyrights at grave risk when they moved pedophiliac priests from parish to parish and even into youth and children's ministries. As one commentator put it, "The crisis in the church is not . . . about pedophilia. Any profession that deals with children will attract some few who would prey upon them. The crisis rather is about a leadership that routinely placed the welfare of the institution—the preservation of appearances, finances, and the status quo—ahead of the welfare of children." In the eyes of those within the church's ministries, children simply lacked a full, embodied reality worthy of protection and care.

Parents and adults at large must take children's rights as enfleshed moral subjects more seriously. What if adults took the time, as Gudorf and recent advocates suggest, to explain to children the differences between appropriate and inappropriate touching and infringement of their bodyright? What if parents explained even seemingly trivial exceptions to the rule, such as when children are asked to undress for the doctor, wear appropriate clothes for certain occasions, or express physical affection to a relative? Offering such explanation may seem a trivial consideration in light of the much larger problems exemplified by the church scandal, but these small considerations lie on the same continuum as gross infringements of sexual abuse. To begin to take children's bodyrights more seriously will require many such small steps.

Among the necessary reforms, Gudorf names changing child-rearing patterns as perhaps "the greatest challenge." Many adults simply assume they have the right to determine children's bodily decisions. Parents often decide what children wear and do, from haircut to shoes, for as much of the duration of childhood as possible, hoping that by doing so they will successfully inculcate their values and beliefs. High school parties and university campuses, known for their big-party atmosphere and dangerously high level of alcoholic consumption, then become an instantaneous experimental opportunity for children to test their sudden release from parental control. Children need instead a gradual transfer of power that involves receiving responsibility for progressively greater choices within a range appropriate to their age and situation.

Part of the problem is that the general public largely presumes that parents are in control of their children, or if they are not, they should be—a view that fits well with the still lingering romantic notions of children as pure and innocent. Captivated by this view, society has infantilized children as fundamentally incapable of constructive thought and action. This has led people to mistake shaping children into socially acceptable adults as the chief task of parenting. Instead, at the center should stand the gradual transfer of appropriate responsibility.

Children actually claim agency, whether parents like it or not, and often to a greater extent than many parents

Children as Agents

want to recognize or admit. Gudorf herself seems somewhat surprised to discover this in the early parenting of her own two disabled children and is adamant, in turn, that people recognize children's power and agency. She and her husband, she states outright, "were never in control" of them; "The children were in control, not only of themselves, but of us" at least as much as they were, dictating "where we went and didn't, what we ate, all home activities, whom we saw, even how much sleep we got." Children even shaped how other adults perceived Gudorf and her husband—as unnecessarily cruel, for example, when they enforced behaviors that appeared harsh to those unknowing adults who observed their parental discipline in public places.

In this ability to shape public perception, children are not entirely innocent of manipulation and distortion. As agents, children are neither entirely virtuous nor entirely depraved. Rather, they are a complex amalgamation of imperfection and potentiality. Even though they are not adults in body or mind, they demand and deserve the kind of recognition usually reserved for adults—that they are full persons trying to learn how to wield power appropriately and how to have a real say in their lives, sometimes to a fault. Some of the real fatigue of parenting comes precisely from having to deal with the constant efforts of children to assert themselves in the myriad decisions that determine their lives, sometimes with good will but not always with such nice intentions.

Without a doubt, this new and more complex view of children as deserving of self-determination presents challenges. Gudorf tries to describe the fine line she draws between enough power and harmful permissiveness. Children should not, for example, "be made to eat when they are not hungry, but neither should they be allowed to consistently substitute nonnutritious snacks for meals. Children should not be made to adopt a parent's dress choices, but neither should they be allowed to wear shorts in the snow."

Finding this middle ground of good-enough parenting is no simple task. Efforts to give children voice certainly make family life much more complicated, and there are limits to the amount of tolerable and appropriate determination. When spending vacation time around my parents, I sometimes catch them exchanging looks at the indecisive quagmire into which my own family sinks as each son voices his opinion about where we are going and what we are going to eat, do, and so on. In general, although we often reserve final veto power, we try to allow them as much say as befits their maturity in daily, even mundane, choices. Sometimes this due process simply leads to paralysis, frustration, and conflict. But sometimes we see the fruits of our tiring family deliberation in signs of maturity and self-confidence. For the most part, we remain willing to live with the perplexity of inviting children into the process because of the conviction that in all the temporary chaos lie seeds for their moral development. As we saw in Chapter Two, children's needs deserve deep respect, but on the other hand they do not always know what they need at each stage of life, much less in minor decisions about what to eat and wear.

Children as Agents

Parents and children must define with care the boundaries of these two equally valid, sometimes competing claims.

Religious communities themselves could play a role in helping parents negotiate these tricky moral waters. If church rituals recognize confirmation or adult baptism for twelve-year-old children as a key step toward adult faith, then churches might also help families foster increased participation by children and youth in family decisions. In general, social justice requires empowering those with lesser power to claim their needs and to work with those who determine whether and how they are met.

Until recent years, church and society have assumed a family model based on the hierarchical power of the father in loving care of those beneath his roof. When the church defended familial rights, it assumed that this also included and benefited children. Children's rights did not need explicit defense. Not only did rights language initially threaten to disrupt this family arrangement, many people feared it would unleash those with greater power to neglect selfishly their responsibility to the more vulnerable, including children.

With the gradual demise of the breadwinner-homemaker marriage and with individuals striving for less hierarchical distribution of power, these assumptions have been questioned. Rights of children have to be extended beyond the one area that social and religious conservatives have championed: arguments for the rights of the unborn. They must include not only rights to care by parents, material support and protection, and rights to education and culture but also rights to safety from abuse, to active involvement of fathers, and to a limitation of absolute parental authority over decisions that threaten children's welfare.

Comprehensive respect for children is not just a right to be guarded and preserved, however. It is a hope and a promise. Paula Cooey paints a wonderful picture of this vision. Her mother was an accomplished dancer who, upon motherhood, turned her energies to teaching dance to kids from lower-middle-class and working families in rural north Georgia. Even at only a dollar per hour for dance and fifty cents for half-hour baton twirling lessons, payment often consisted of an imaginative exchange of nonmonetary goods and services, from home produce to costumes for recitals. On the least of means, her mother could lure "even the most cynical," the most hard up, or the clumsiest little boy or girl into tripping across the stage with pirouettes, twirls, and leaps.

This, nevertheless, was not the essence of what was learned. Children gained a confidence "through bodily discipline and practice" and, moreover, an embodied joy. Cooey's real intent is to explore the religious nature of such joy, but her essay conveys a powerful message: Christians are obliged to create a world in which "every child who wants might learn to dance." Dance becomes a metaphor for a joy-filled engagement with life that defies injustice. Her mother bequeaths to her the wisdom of women working together for justice, quietly subverting oppressive social structures in their own small ways. Elsewhere in a book on the family, Cooey states this premise more formally: "Christians need to be at the forefront of advocating for the protection of all children, regardless of what kind of household, religious or otherwise, they come from."

CHILDREN AS SPIRITUAL AGENTS

Feminist theology makes especially unique contributions in one final area. Children's moral agency deserves protection and support precisely because of their role as spiritual beings. Seeing children as spiritual stands over against a long Christian history that has largely stripped them of such agency. Even those classical theologians who advocated developmental understanding still pictured children as generally passive recipients of church teachings. To claim children as active spiritual participants also goes beyond the typical thrust in the recent surge of popular books that promote the spirituality of everyday life but quickly bypass children. Finally, seeing children as spiritual agents adds an overlooked dimension to the affirmation of children as ends in themselves among secular spokespersons who seldom connect this to children's spiritual capacity.

For the majority of Western Christian spiritual history, a wide gap has stood between secular worldliness and the sacredness of otherworldly communion with God. Children, and other related earthly concerns, generally impeded genuine contemplation and spiritual attainment. To conceive, bear, and rear children simply immersed one too directly in carnality, triviality, and transmission of sin to have much positive spiritual consequence. Although some monasteries provided education and took in young children, children were not a source of revelation by any stretch of the imagination. Early fathers of the church, such as Jerome, instead associated procreation and the love of children with "shame and sorrow." Celibacy was a purer route to the love of God. People naturally came to see prayer as something one does in the private inner room of the soul, away from all the noise and busyness of external life. Even prominent spiritual leaders today continue to associate spirituality with solitude and silence—two precious commodities, when one has children.

Feminist theology calls this vision of spirituality into question. Dismissing material conditions—the messiness of daily life—in defining ideal spirituality has left us with two big problems in relationship to children: limited models for understanding children as a source of religious knowledge, and limited models for understanding parenting as a religious practice. Adult spirituality must be reimagined precisely in relationship to new views of children's spiritual role.

Declarations about children as a source of revelation in feminist theology are quite bold. Couture, for example, firmly asserts that connections with children are "a means of grace, a vehicle through which God makes God's self known." God appears in the faces of vulnerable children helped in times of need. Gudorf says that her experience

Children as Agents

of her own children has been "basic" for her understanding of human nature. Religion scholar Kathryn Rabuzzi's entire project on mothering could be summarized as an effort to proclaim that motherhood has a sacred dimension. To be a mother is, in her words, "to be 'graced.'"

I am a little less certain about this. In my own exploration in *Also a Mother,* I admit, "having children has forever changed my ways of knowing and thinking." But "parting the passions in order to articulate those ways comes less easily." In another characteristically ambivalent moment, I write that "nothing has ever subverted my peace of mind as has living according to the pace of my small sons, and yet nothing has ever taught me as much about myself and my location in the world." Children promise delight, bewilderment, and enlightenment, certainly. But caution in stating what children reveal is warranted. Undiscriminating assertions run the risk of romanticizing and idolizing children, stigmatizing those unable to bear or care for them, and overlooking the possibly harsh realities of child care and the many times in which children do not promote revelatory insight.

These caveats, however, should not keep us from teasing out what children make known, and even from speculating about what God might be making known through them. Children can evoke new energy even as they demand energy, sometimes sparking fresh engagement, enhanced creativity, and even religious awe before life itself. Young children in particular challenge the thoughtlessly hurried pace and aim of adult striving. They see what adults have ceased to notice. They are prone to say what they see, at least early on. (When we first went to a major league baseball game with one of my young sons who played on a co-ed tee-ball team, he asked, "Where are the women?" Right after we moved from Chicago to Nashville, another son questioned, "Why are all the workers in this restaurant African American, but none of the customers?") They greet the world's creations—moon, water, sand, fireflies, thunderstorms—with a certain respect, intrigue, and religious wonder. They also ask fundamental religious and philosophical questions (like the night one son wondered, "What was here before God?" as I tucked him in, or the young girl at church who asserted that she "didn't think a loving God would allow for hell"). Indeed, misconceptions of children as innocent, cute, and innocuous have often misled adults into teaching children "to reject their epiphanies," as Kathleen Norris laments. (In fact, some church members were disturbed that the minister did not correct the girl's perceptions about God and hell.) People seem genuinely surprised to discover that children actually think provocatively. One philosopher who has written about children as philosophers remarks—not without some astonishment—they "even engage in reasoning that professional philosophers can recognize as philosophical."

Many women theologians do not find this startling in the least. Children have had an unprecedented role in informing theological reflection. Anglican theologian Margaret Hebblethwaite devotes an entire book to how children inform reflection on God. In having children, women may experience a twofold dynamic that she describes as "finding God in motherhood" and "finding motherhood in God." Reflecting on her own situation as a mother of three small children, she shows "how God can bring meaning to the experience, and the experience can bring meaning to God."

Mothering evokes a range of new ways to think about God: through the child's weight in her womb, that God is even closer to us than most images presume; through her captivation by children's charming quirks, that God finds our very gaucheness endearing; through the tedium of daily caregiving routines, that God finds ways to bridge both the idealism of the past and the disillusionment of the present; through endurance of a child's inconsolable storms, that God remains ever present despite our distress; and through her desperation in the midst of her children's demands, that in God lies rest and refreshment. The frustrations of daily life with small children also lead to new ways of thinking about spirituality in the midst of domestic work. Problems with conception teach humility before God's creative power; labor and delivery teach trust; and children bring simultaneous joy, frustration, and desperation that hint at the mystery of God's love for us and our necessary reliance upon it in raising children.

These insights point to a spirituality of children and parenthood that challenges a powerful stream in the Christian tradition that has rendered children, parenting, and parental sexuality less conducive to religious experience than the celibate life. Catholic scholar Wendy Wright has been especially instrumental in questioning a tradition in which "few of the great remembered prayers [pray-ers] of our tradition were married," "few had children," and many thought spiritual ascension meant transcending one's body, leaving one's family to journey to somewhere else, and entering a life of voluntary poverty. For those who care for children, spirituality arises in the midst of the complexities of intimate attachments; in the busyness and world-maintaining activities of homemaking; in the self-transcending powers of sexual intercourse, pregnancy, childbirth, and nursing; and in providing for physical needs and stewardship of material possessions. Similarly, historical theologian Elizabeth Dreyer names parenting the "ascetic opportunity *par excellence*." In a manner comparable to, but distinct from, the monastic in seclusion, a parent encounters unexpected opportunities to practice the disciplined religiosity that lies at the heart of asceticism's loving self-denial: "A full night's sleep, time to oneself, the freedom to come and go as one pleases—all this must be given up. . . . Huge chunks of life are laid down at the behest of infants. And then, later, parents must let go."

Children call for the practice of something that I have described as "contemplation in the midst of chaos." The very terms *chaos* and *contemplation* need to be rethought. Contemplation is too often collapsed into a removed state of quiescence, and chaos is seen as a negative or even evil state to be avoided at all costs. The conventional script calls for a choice: either contemplation or chaos, not both.

With children, these preconceptions are inadequate. Children warrant a spirituality that emerges out of disruption, interruption, and confusion. Genuine contemplation, defined as an attentiveness that alters one's

Children as Agents

way of seeing, can occur in a number of situations, chaotic or not. Attending to children in such a way that one is altered is precisely a key ingredient of good parenting. Life's busyness, therefore, is not an utterly secular wasteland; limited perceptions of spirituality and children have hidden the possibility of God's presence in the clutter and mess. Meaning can emerge *in* the chaos.

As companion to solitude and silence, contemplation in the midst of chaos rests on relational connection and authentic conversation as avenues to the sacred. Rather than thinking one must give up prayer when one births a baby, or turn it over to others, one finds prayer in the oddest of situations. Years ago, while changing diapers (as bizarre as it sounds), I sometimes felt curiously attuned, even spiritually grounded, despite or perhaps because of the intimacy connected to the grungy aspects of the chore. Prayer is transformed in the midst of the flurry of family activity. Finding a place of rest amid the cacophony of demands requires a discipline oriented around the incidentals, the disruptions, and the routines. Single words and short prayers must counteract domestic life's dissipation. One has to capitalize on moments of frustration that fill the hours of care, when a rush of anger leads one to curse, by taking a "second breath," as one writer counsels, and recognizing the curse as hiding an impulse "however darkly . . . to pray." Frustration and irritation can be seen for what they could become: an invitation to let in another way of seeing the situation.

All this is not to say that contemplation in the midst of chaos is ideal, or that eight days of silence in a Jesuit retreat center do not have personal appeal and an important place. In fact, the ability to sustain oneself in the midst of chaos draws deeply upon what one learns in moments akin to monastic silence. Rather, just as the opposition between pilgrimage and home is an unhelpful dichotomy, silence and solitude do not exhaust the avenues of spiritual renewal and, when taken as exhaustive, render other avenues invisible and neglected. Life with children demands that spiritual disciplines of long-standing value, such as silence, solitude, and pilgrimage, be reconnected to their companion practices of conversation, connection, and homemaking.

Neither the church nor Christian scholarship has supported a spiritual practice that reclaims domestic chaos or frustration as a viable source of divine encounter. In general, religious traditions and the academy are afraid to celebrate biological life processes, child care, and children as occasion for spiritual growth. That parenthood involves change for the parent as well as the child is also a relatively new idea for developmental psychology. The well-known psychologist Daniel Stern, for example, is quick to admit that, despite his training and work with children, motherhood as a process of birth for the mother as well as the child is an entirely new idea for him. Prominent mental health studies assume that parenthood requires little change in parental mind-set and that parental growth has little role in the development of children.

Religious feminists testify that this is not the case. Some, such as Rabuzzi, argue that childbirth in particular is a powerfully transformative spiritual event in women's lives that men have "stolen" and appropriated into male-dominated rituals and symbols. Giving birth sparks a threefold process of simultaneously dying to oneself as previously known, being born anew, and giving birth to a child. It offers the potential of a genuinely ecstatic experience, a reality from which Christianity has shied away. Biblical scholar Tikva Frymer-Kensky also believes birth processes ought to be better celebrated as "occasions for spiritual growth and communication with the divine." Frustrated by the lack of religious childbirth literature, she retrieves birth incantations from such sources as ancient Sumerian and Akkadian texts, the Jewish prayer tradition, and prayer books from eighteenth-century Italy. Her colleagues and readers themselves may be surprised to discover religious traditions that so deeply value childbirth and mark it as especially promising for deepening spiritual life.

Parents' continued growth beyond childbirth, including facing and resolving leftover issues with their own parents, has a tremendous impact on children. In reflections on her parenting, Gudorf discovers, for example, that her need to control her first son during his teens simply projected upon her son her own childhood and adolescent struggles for freedom from her overly controlling parents. Recognizing this allowed her to quit working out her problems through her parenting of him. Perhaps the biggest and sometimes least suspected change happens in the couple itself, as each parent continuously assumes new roles in relationship to the child, becomes absorbed to a differing degree in a child's care, and hence experiences new and sometimes disturbing dynamics in relationship to the other as parents.

Under all circumstances, as difficult as it is, the parental role must be, as Gudorf remarks, "a constantly diminishing one in the life of a child." This does not mean that parents become less important or less close to their children. Rather, children may initially meet most of their needs through the parents, but parents cannot depend on children alone to meet their needs; they require other sources of support and fulfillment. Although this advice seems obvious, parental overidentification and merger with children are, as we have seen, a difficult temptation. Letting go of children goes against the grain of human self-preservation precisely because to let go means to admit one's own finitude, limits, and fears. For a religious person, perhaps the hardest spiritual lesson, or the most difficult virtue, to acquire through care of children is entrusting oneself and those most loved to God's care and protection. It is only such trust that finally allows one to stop short of using one's children to build up oneself. Entrusting one's children to God thwarts the temptation to overidentify and overinvest. This claim points to a final ramification of reimagining children as spiritual agents, to which I return in the Epilogue: the assertion of care of children as a religious practice and community discipline.

CHILDREN RECONSTRUCTED

Feminist theological constructions of children as the labor of love and as moral and spiritual agents add significant nuance to our attempts to grapple with knowing children. Behind these views stand an experiential grasp of children's vulnerability before the adults that create and shape their world. Children number among the "least of these" (Matt. 25:40). They suffer from the same kind of social dismissal and Victorian romanticization faced by women. Yet they are moral and spiritual equals, owed comparable respect and concern as to adults (and perhaps greater), given their temporary dependence and vulnerability. When rights and needs conflicts, those most vulnerable—usually children—deserve preferential treatment.

In contrast to some Christian views of children and sin, a feminist theology of sin pertains as much to the social sphere of oppression as to personal acts. It is something to which children fall victim more than something they engage in as culprits. Children may harbor sinful thoughts, but the depth and extent of their corrupt behavior is usually in direct proportion to the actions of the adults in their midst. Feminist theology has defined sexism, or anything that leads to women's disparagement, as sinful. But reimagining children warrants naming "adultism," or anything that causes children's diminution, as sinful. Because they possess such incredulous trust and love for parents, sometimes in the midst of the most horrible circumstances, they stand in need of adult advocacy and parental protection.

At the same time, children hold more power over their parents than is commonly believed. Children are gifts of God's good creation, and even if not yet adults they are, as Cooey claims, "persons rather than property of their parents, and as persons, worthy of rights and capable of taking responsibility commensurate with their

LET THE CHILDREN COME

development." These views challenge sentimentalized notions and portray children as gradually responsible human actors, not victims, but subjects themselves, deserving of the kind of empowerment, liberation, inclusivity, and justice sought for women.

This exploration suggests the need to reconcile two critical values often seen as competing: children's welfare *and* women's well-being. Keeping women's welfare in mind is especially imperative in a national and international context in which women are still deprived of fundamental freedoms in child-bearing and gender roles. In many places, women do not have the right to make decisions about marriage, sex, work, and contraception. Nor do they have respect for their bodies, control over them, or mutuality rather than domination in sexual intercourse. The heavy responsibilities for child care and housework are often not shared.

Only as these aspects of women's well-being are addressed will children's well-being improve. The Christian ethicist Beverly Harrison sees this double agenda as precisely the task of feminist Christian ethics. It must "contribute to that almost endless reconstruction of inherited moral traditions in a direction that seeks to assume that women's well-being genuinely matters and that the well-being of the children that women bear matter[s]." These two conjoint concerns define the parameters of Christian responsibility and, if logically extended, actually include the "well-being of everybody."

Expectations about balancing these two norms sometimes seem idealistic. There are and will remain insurmountable conflicts and friction between mothers' and children's needs. As Harrison willingly admits elsewhere, "The social policy I propose is highly utopic. Even to imagine a society that would function to prevent a trade-off between fetal life and women's well-being is difficult." For feminist theology, then, the ideal of securing the welfare of both groups must be placed into a fertile Christian eschatological framework. Bringing the ideal to fruition rests at least partly on faith—an "assurance of things hoped for, the conviction of things not seen" (Heb.11:1). A faith that non-Christians often find so disconcerting serves its purpose in keeping the challenge in front of us. Simply put, religious feminists will continue to imagine a redemptive society in which "every child might learn to dance" and children and adults might learn to twirl together.

EPILOGUE

Care of Children as a
Religious Discipline and
Community Practice

———

The most inspirational point in my reflection on this book came at an unexpected time and in an unexpected place. Along with a dozen students and three other faculty, I had reached the shores of the Pacific coast of Nicaragua as part of a two-and-a-half-week travel seminar led by the Center for Global Education. Nicaragua is the second poorest nation in the American hemisphere, and U.S. political and economic policies are partly to blame. In the 1980s, when hope-filled Nicaraguan revolutionaries successfully overthrew a long-standing dictatorial dynasty supported by the United States and created programs for land redistribution, education, and health services, the Reagan-Bush administration began a decade of warfare against the new government, perceived as a communist threat.

How a country no larger than New York state and only a half-day's trip from the United States could be so economically impoverished and seen as such a danger was a question that plagued all of us from the beginning. Even setting foot on a plane to Managua filled not with Nicaraguans (most of whom lack resources for international travel) but with do-good U.S. mission groups in matching T-shirts forced me to wonder about my role as a U.S. native in perpetuating such drastic economic and social inequities. Most U.S. citizens do not even know, for example, that the United States has intervened militarily in Nicaragua five times since 1850, most recently in the 1980s in support of the counterrevolutionaries. I didn't have a clue. Nor could most of us explain why our per capita gross domestic product is $29,683 while the Nicaraguan GDP is $452, especially given Nicaragua's considerable natural resources. It is hard to dodge the conclusion that U.S. imperialistic exploitation is at least one major factor.

By the time we reached Poneloya Beach, we had listened to many people talk from different perspectives about how Nicaraguan hopes were dashed on the shore of economic and political turmoil. We were expecting to hear Pinita Gurdian Vijil speak on her experiences as a Christian in the Revolution. As it turned out, however, she spoke not only as a Christian but also as a Christian parent. Raised in a wealthy family in a country where one cannot easily avoid contact with the poor, she and her husband faced a fundamental turning point in the 1980s when they had to decide where they would stand. They chose to give up the security of their social position and joined the movement that challenged a government built upon acquisition of personal wealth and power.

What was most striking to me, however, was Pinita's understanding of her role as a parent and the support she received from the faith community. Initiating regular family meetings, she and her husband intentionally chose to engage their children in the religious and moral questions they faced about how to live well—that is, how to pursue justice and compassion for the poor—in times of great strife and inequity. Notably, without their involvement in a lay movement for renovation in the Catholic church and participation in a small Christian base community, they would have struggled to do any of this. Their children, like themselves and not unlike the U.S. visitors listening to her, had grown up presuming the benefits of their social class—paid help in the home, education abroad, good health and nutrition, and few limits on material possessions. Yet when they invited their children into discussion about their political and religious commitment, they found the children eager to embrace the same questions that worried them: Why do we have so much and others so little? More essentially, how do we change our lives and participate in change?

As it turned out, Pinita's children were ready to live with less so others could have more. A prayer for her children, published in one of the national newspapers in the late 1970s, epitomizes the seriousness with which she regarded her children and the gravity with which she perceived parenting as a religious task and a community practice. She wanted her children to know that "people should not be valued by the measure or the extent to which they can make money." The prayer captures her hopes to raise "brave and determined children" who know their own fallibility and dependence on God, aspire to freedom and self-respect but not at the expense of the good of the other, and are not ruled by material possessions but seek a fair and just society.

Can we U.S. citizens, often hampered by our opulence, clear space for this kind of serious conversation with our children and conscientious grappling with the cause of children and the mandate of parenting? Does it take, I wondered, political and social struggle to wrestle forth from human nature such deep engagement in parenting as a religious practice? What would happen if religious congregations called parents to sit down and write out such a statement of intention and hope with regard to their own children? Would parents have to think twice about the typical U.S. prayer—"I just want my child to be happy"—and seek a deeper conviction and cause than the alternatives of happiness and unhappiness?

Thinking about children as embodying sin, gift, work, and agency suggests fertile alternative convictions about what adults might ask from and for children, beyond happiness. It also opens up a fresh avenue to discuss the radical understanding of parenting as a religious discipline and community practice. Children need, from women and men of faith, care that respects them as persons, regards them as capable of good and bad, values them as gifts, appreciates them as demanding of serious labor, and views them as agents. These are not needs that a parent can or ought to face alone. The practice of raising children belongs to all Christians, and not solely to parents or to mothers. In the whole feminist theological corpus on motherhood, the common good, and social justice, one of the most striking commonalities among the three groups is promotion of what might be called "non-parent-parenting." The ability to care for children and to maintain a balance between self-sacrifice and self-love in relationship to them depends on wider circles of care that extend beyond the immediate biological or adoptive parents. It is no wonder, therefore, that in pursuit of just love in families a great deal of feminist theological attention has gone toward securing these wider supports.

Womanist theologians—African American women who challenge both black liberationists and feminist theologians to stretch the categories of analysis to include racism and sexism—have most explicitly promoted traditions of "othermothering" within congregations and communities. "Othermothers"—grandmothers, sisters, aunts, cousins, and neighbors—share the right and responsibility to discipline children and secure their welfare. Children are not private property to be disposed of as parents would like; they need a more generic kind of social mothering that extends well beyond biological mothers and depends upon the willingness of nonbiologically related adults to adopt children as a primary responsibility. Caring for children in this view refers to much more than mere physical labor with economic and political meanings. Indeed, it is explicitly named a religious duty incumbent upon people, whether they are literally parents or not.

Two distinct Christian practices repeatedly surface in this discussion that are particularly relevant to supporting children and parents in the face of sexual, economic, and political injustice and hardship: adoption and godparenting. Recognition of children as active participants in the family requires reclaiming these two traditional Christian themes.

A friend and colleague, Jeanne Stevenson Moessner, brought to my attention the theological neglect of and social embarrassment about adoption. Christianity has largely forgotten its preeminence as a crucial theological theme. The doctrine of justification, favored by Lutherans, and the doctrine of sanctification, promoted by Methodists, have overshadowed adoption. On a more personal level, saying one's child is adopted is stereotypically seen as admitting some kind of failure.

Yet adoption is a primary spiritual category and practice. In fact, paradigmatically it represents the path by which all Christians enter God's family. Some Christian traditions have prized adoption as a theological doctrine, exemplified perhaps in the Westminster Confession of Faith, where claims about adoption are situated right between claims about justification and sanctification. Standing on par with both of these, the theme of adoption acknowledges the status of all God's children as literally adoptees into the divine family, loved not out of inheritance but through God's invitation into community. Adoption, a distinctive idea in both Hebrew and Christian scriptures, is not, however, just a metaphor. The metaphor in turn invites radical practice. Christians are called to transcend common biological loyalties and extend the same generosity of spirit toward children not their own.

This does not mean simply adopting when one cannot procreate. It includes working to create a covenant of extrabiological, extralegal kinship with children in need. But the spirit and doctrine of adoption means even more than this. As Christians strengthen the bonds internal to their own families, they must actively subsume promotion of family interests under the greater imperative to love one's neighbor and care for the poor.

Similarly, the practice of godparenting, built around the very idea of adoption, needs reinvigoration. It has acquired a superficial character among many mainstream North American Christians, sometimes lacking its previous connotations of serious responsibility for spiritual oversight and material care. Only some Christian denominations continue the practice. Besides the token honor of being named a godparent, responsibilities might encompass parents' growing needs and include a variety of supports, such as training in parental skills, sustained mentoring with new parents, and intervention in times of crisis.

In other words, feminist theology suggests that adult spirituality in relationship to children calls for a distinctive kind of personal discipline and community practice. A range of scholars put the personal desire to have children and the moral obligation to extend altruistic care to all children together as companion considerations. Child bearing is not, in Beverly Harrison's words, "a purely capricious, individualistic matter," but a complex, demanding activity accountable to the moral claims of the wider community. Parenthood is, as Catholic ethicist Lisa Sowle Cahill asserts, a "specifically *sexual* mode of social participation."

As Cahill sees it, the family is neither a "haven from the world" nor "a nexus of social control" but a "school for critical contribution to the social good" in which parents and children alike learn how to contribute to society. Although families naturally seek their own well-being, the "most distinctively Christian moral virtue" is seeking the well-being of those beyond the boundaries of the natural family. Interestingly enough, Cahill herself is deeply formed by the theme and practice of adoption, even though she spends little time talking about it explicitly. She notes in the preface of one book that behind her reflections stands her own experience of raising three children from Thailand in addition to two biological children, her sister's work as foster mother and mother of three adopted children, and friendships with gays and lesbians who have adopted "hard to place" children.

The issue is therefore not simply what the wider community owes parents and children but also what families owe the wider community. Children, in other words, are not an extension of the parent's self; instead, they extend the family toward greater commitment to the common good of which children are a crucial part. Caring for children can actually tie adults into life in a new way. As one Nicaraguan revolutionary wrote to her young daughter, "A mother isn't just someone who gives birth and cares for her child. A mother feels the pain of all children, of all peoples, as if they had been born from her womb." Although this exaggerates natural parental benevolence to make a point, giving birth and caring for an infant can elicit a new way of seeing each person as someone else's child. To learn to nurture through parenting can as a consequence potentially teach an essential human virtue and even deepen one's life of faith. To care for children, and not simply one's own, then becomes the key to the good Christian life. This is why, for many feminist theologians, social disregard for children in general amounts to a spiritual crisis on the part of adults.

Many of these ideas fly in the face of what the dominant culture believes about children, parents, and families. The prevailing ethic is that one should look after one's own skin (literally) regardless of the good of the other. The prevailing spirituality is that people determine their own destiny. A Christian ethic of children, by contrast, asserts that one's own good is inextricably linked to the common good, the good of others, the good of the whole. A Christian spirituality reminds adults that, in the end, people do not determine their own destiny or that of their children. Children come from God and to God they return. Life's value is not measured in tangible terms, by whom or what our children know or what they accomplish. The good lies in the reign of God and the love of neighbor.

These ideas and the practices embodying them—that individual good is inextricably linked to the good of others and that nothing matters in the end as much as the praise and love of God—may not be ideas people like to hear. They are neither simple to preach nor easy to practice. If Christianity says what it really needs to say about children, it may make people uncomfortable. But more important, reimagining children from a Christian perspective should encourage much greater care when tossing around claims that children are gifts or children are work. With these and other views, Christianity has essential countercultural values with regard to children, love, and grace that it must continue to offer. After all, the moment the disciples start to debate their pecking order, Jesus paradoxically says several times in different ways in all three Synoptic gospels, "Let the first become the last ... whoever is least among you is the one who is great." In one instance, he takes a child in his arms.

THINKING ABOUT
CHILDREN AND FAITH

Questions for Reflection

———

In the following pages, you will find a list of reflection and discussion questions for each chapter. These questions are geared toward individual or group reflection for parents, caregivers, students, or anyone concerned with constructing a theological understanding of children. They invite you to think about both the personal and communal implications of the material introduced in each chapter. Each question is reflective and open ended. Some may prompt you to record responses in a personal journal; others will provoke you to engage in dialogue with others about the issues raised in the book. The questions can also be used to guide group discussions about childhood and children. In particular, "Activities for Group Interaction" are simple learning processes created to help active and visual learners participate in the reflection and discussion. Leaders can use them either to begin or to conclude group discussions. Some require advance reflection and preparation.

INTRODUCTION AND AUTHOR'S NOTE

1. What "instructions" do you most wish had come with the children in your care?
2. What do you see as the biggest challenge for parents and caregivers of children in the twenty-first century?
3. What assumptions or values about children and childhood do you bring to this discussion? Who and what do you think shaped those assumptions and values?
4. Do you agree that middle-class U.S. parents are extraordinarily focused on the welfare of their own individual children? Why or why not? Do you see any connection between the heightened pace of middle-class children's lives and the lack of opportunities for working and underclass children?
5. How has Christianity portrayed children? Do you see Christianity as a relevant resource in child rearing or in contesting cultural images of children? What about religious communities, psychology, or feminism?
6. A feminist maternal theology shapes this book. Review the four directions or assumptions that such an approach provides (p. 6, Author's Note)

and discuss how each might question cultural assumptions about children.

7. What do you imagine should be included in "a bolder Christian vision of children"?

Activity for Group Interaction

Distribute magazines and newspapers to participants and invite them to pick out images of children. What do these media portrayals tell you about cultural values placed on children? How does your faith tradition and community of belief challenge the views of children reflected in these media images? Can you think of ways that scripture and history may also challenge these portrayals?

CHAPTER ONE

––––

1. How does the chapter's history of childhood surprise you and alter your assumptions about childhood?
2. Should children be compensated for their work around the house? Why or why not? How do you think the shift from asset to burden in the household economy has impacted children themselves?
3. What do you perceive as the upside of highly valuing children emotionally? Is there a downside for children themselves or for others who support the system of lavishing care, attention, and material wealth on children? Why or why not?

4. What have you noticed about children that supports the idea that they are depraved or innocent? Do you agree that the shift away from moral and religious training to emotional nurture increased the pressure on parents or robbed children of agency? Why or why not?

5. Do you agree that children are less innocent and yet more vulnerable than presupposed by modernity? How do you think assumptions about childhood purity affected teens or adults?

6. In the past, reconfiguration of our understanding of children has evoked discomfort; what is it about reimagining the "knowing child" or the imperfect, potentially volatile child in an imperfect, volatile world that evokes fear, frustration, or anxiety in you?

7. Which biblical resources (for example, biblical stories, parables, and proverbs) and cultural resources (self-help books, media reports, and the like) shape your thinking about the nature of children? Does religious or theological language inform your thinking in any way?

Activity for Group Interaction

Obtain a copy of the book *Pictures of Innocence,* by Anne Higonnet, from a local library or bookstore. Reproduce for group discussion pictures that show the adultlike children of pre-Enlightenment painters, the innocent children of the last few centuries, and the knowing children of more recent times. Discuss the reactions and thoughts that these different portraits evoke in light of the chapter's exploration of the changes in cultural constructions of children.

Thinking About Children and Faith

Chapter Two

1. Do you think psychology has replaced religion in constructing the nature of childhood? What of genuine significance have you learned about children or about yourself as a child from psychology? Has psychology helped you do a better job of loving children?

2. In what ways have you noticed yourself or other parents using children to meet narcissistic needs? What about the culture at large?

3. Which Christian beliefs have been most challenged by modern psychology? For example, how does psychology question Christian views of punishment, self-sacrifice, and self-love? What is your judgment about the validity of these critiques?

4. Christianity also challenges psychology. In what ways does psychology come up short in its understandings of children and parents?

5. What does your faith tradition say about the nature of human failure and wrongdoing? How does this influence the way you conceive of children and child rearing?

6. How do you think Christian concepts of sin and grace, confession and forgiveness, reconciliation, discernment, prayer and worship might enrich understandings of childhood and parenting practices?

7. Psychologists such as Alice Miller and Heinz Kohut have explored the importance of healthy narcissism or self-love. Compare this idea with

the Hebrew Bible commandment in Leviticus 19:18 and Deuteronomy 6:4–5, repeated by Jesus in Luke 10:27, to love your neighbor as yourself.

Activity for Group Interaction

In preparation for class, invite participants to visit a local bookstore, look at what kinds of books about children are on the shelves and the best-seller list, write down several popular titles, and make notes of common themes in the tables of contents. In particular, focus on books in the psychology and religion sections of the store. In class, discuss observations. How is the child commonly portrayed by psychology, religion, or other fields? What do group members think about these portrayals?

CHAPTER THREE

1. Do you react negatively to the idea of children as sinful? Do the illustrations from Augustine, Simons, Edwards, and others persuade you that sin is a useful theological category for understanding children's lives? Why or why not?
2. Do you agree with the chapter's argument that Christian views of sin do not inherently lead to abuse and can be read in ways that empower children and parents? Why or why not?
3. The Christian tradition assumes that for children to develop morally and spiritually, they need faithful adults within supportive communities.

Thinking About Children and Faith

How does your family or faith community provide such support to parents and children for this difficult process?

4. When you think of discipline, do you associate it more with punishment or teaching? How should parents respond to knowing misdeeds or unacceptable behavior by children? What strategies have you observed or found effective for instilling responsibility in children?

5. Menno Simons and Augustine each offer theological reflection about children in relation to different views of infant baptism. How does your tradition connect its understanding of childhood and adulthood with its theology of baptism?

6. What sayings of Jesus and other biblical stories or imperatives come to mind when you think about the spiritual development of children? Do these guide your thinking about children?

Activity for Group Interaction

Gather together your congregational or denominational statements about baptism. Make copies for the group. Articulate together the assumed theology within and behind these statements. Discuss what this theology says about the following: sin and salvation, the nature of children, the nature of spiritual and moral change, children as innocent or sinful, and ways to nurture or raise children in faith. How effectively does your congregation enact in its community life the sentiments assumed by baptismal ceremonies and the words spoken within them?

CHAPTER FOUR

---

1. How do you see culture at large and the church specifically tempted to think about or treat children as product, consumer, burden, or means to larger economic ends? What strategies do you use for resisting such temptations?

2. Have you said or heard people say that children are gifts? Did the claim hold any specific religious or moral meanings? What experiences with children have you had that would confirm the specifically moral and religious meanings behind the phrase?

3. Think of times when children you know or have heard stories about served as exemplary disciples of Christ. What did you learn from the words or actions of these children that helps you in your own life of faith?

4. Compare the different theological understandings of children in the household codes (Eph. 5:22–6:9; Col. 3:18–4:1) and the sayings and actions of Jesus (Mark 10:13–16). How do you reconcile these two views?

5. Read stories of Jesus welcoming, blessing, and healing children in Matthew 18:1–5, Mark 9:14–29, Luke 8:40–56, John 6:1–14. In what ways do these words and actions of Jesus turn the first-century view of children upside down? The twenty-first century view of children?

6. How can children be both models for Christian discipleship and objects of Christian ministry? Discuss the theological significance of children as both gift and task.

Activity for Group Interaction

This chapter has offered a wide variety of social and theological portrayals of children. At one extreme, children can be understood as an ultimate gift sent by God in Christ. At the other extreme, they are portrayed as an ultimate burden and are exploited as a means to an end (war, sex, work). Write these two extreme views on construction paper and display them at opposite ends of a wall in your discussion area. Provide sheets of construction paper, markers, and tape, and invite participants to write down and display other portrayals of children from the chapter (for example, welcomed by Jesus, consumers, objects of the household codes, and so on). Use the resulting visual descriptions of children to begin your discussion.

Chapter Five

---

1. What assumptions do you have about feminist views of children? Does this chapter change or modify them?
2. A good deal of the actual work of rearing children is hidden. In your experience of being a child or a parent, who did you observe doing this work? What problems did this cause? What do you assume about the roles of mothers, fathers, and other family members?
3. Some feminists argue that child rearing should be more fairly shared. What strategies for shared parenting have you seen work well?

4. In what ways does your religious tradition value self-sacrifice? Are the expectations different for men and women or for parents and children? How do these values impact the ideals of "good parenting" in your faith community or congregation?
5. How do you envision a love for children that involves sacrifice but aims at mutuality? How do you imagine the process of change and growth that this vision presumes? What limits to mutual love might be encountered along the way? What rewards?
6. What might a "good hierarchy" look like? How might a "transitional hierarchy"—one aiming toward mutuality—be enacted in families over time?

Activity for Group Interaction

Just the word *feminism* often elicits strong feelings and opinions. To diffuse some of the intensity, put the word *feminism* up on a poster or marker board. Ask participants to offer first a list of negative cultural images of feminism, then to move to more positive images. Acknowledge the differences of opinion and feeling, and invite openness and respect toward each other and for the discussion ahead. To conclude, on another poster or marker board try to list what the chapter identified as some of feminist theology's positive contributions to the understanding of children.

CHAPTER SIX

———

1. Have you thought much about the idea of children as agents? In what ways do you think adults have failed to take children seriously or failed to allow children adequate say about their lives?
2. If the idea of children as agents were to be more fully implemented by your family, congregation, or larger faith community, what policies or practices might have to be changed?
3. Why do you think adults have tended to overlook the "bodyright" of children?
4. What practices have you seen or attempted that are effective in making a gradual transfer of responsibility from parents to children?
5. The chapter argues that as agents, "children are neither entirely virtuous nor entirely depraved. Rather, they are a complex amalgamation of imperfection and potentiality." What is most challenging for you about viewing childhood agency in this way?
6. Following Hebblethwaite's reflections, in your experience how have children enriched the meaning of God for you, and how has God enriched the meaning of children for you?
7. In what ways do you think of child rearing as a spiritual practice? What forms might the practice of prayer take in caring for infants? Children? Teens? Adult children?

Thinking About Children and Faith

Activity for Group Interaction

To begin a discussion, create a line on the floor with masking tape to divide the discussion area into two equal parts. Stand at one end of the line and ask participants to line up on the masking tape and to face you. Then read the following pairs of statements or ideas, and ask participants to indicate their preference for one or the other by moving away from the line to the right or left. They should indicate the strength of their preference about each statement by moving farther away from the middle. After reading each pair, stop and ask one volunteer from each side to say why he or she preferred one statement over the other. (There are no right or wrong answers!)

Move left *if you prefer:*	*Move* right *if you prefer:*
Spiritual life as going on a journey	Spiritual life as coming home
Silence and solitude	Contemplation in chaos
A week alone at a retreat center	A week on a family vacation
Children have rights	Children have needs
Children should be responsible	Children should be protected
Children must be taught what is right	Children must be allowed to claim agency
Children are virtuous	Children are depraved
Children need more guidance and restriction	Children need more freedom and permission
Respect for children is a right	Respect for children is a promise

Thinking About Children and Faith

God reveals much about children	Children reveal much about God

EPILOGUE

—

Having read this book's reflection on children from a theological perspective, how are you thinking about children differently? What ideas have been most challenging? Most helpful? Most dramatic? How has reading this book changed the way you think about children as sinful and as gift, as the labor of love and as agents?

1. What prayers do you find yourself praying for the children in your spheres of influence?
2. What might it mean for you to take on the spiritual practice and religious discipline of adoption or godparenting in the community of faith to which you belong? What would it mean for your family, congregation, or larger faith community to take these religious practices seriously? How do you think such practices might enrich the lives of children you know? How might it enrich your own life?
3. How do you strike a balance between providing for the needs of your family and serving the needs of impoverished children in your community and globally? Similarly, how do you negotiate the competing needs of what families can expect from a wider community and what a wider community can expect from parents and children?

4. How do you teach your children to become persons of faith and to engage the larger Christian community and a world of need? What role do you hope the church will play in this formational process?
5. What religious practices or disciplines do you think would be most helpful in the rearing of children?

Activity for Group Interaction

Take what you have learned through your reading and discussion, as well as the wisdom of your own faith tradition, and formulate a confessional statement about children. Consider asking for input from children in your church as well. Such a statement could be shared with your wider community of faith, celebrated in worship, or presented to church members, or it could become an impetus to more faithful and theologically rich discussions and practices of welcoming, nurturing, and serving children and parents.

Thinking About Children and Faith

REFERENCES

AUTHOR'S NOTE

My own early work on mothering to which I refer is *Also a Mother: Work and Family as Theological Dilemma* (Nashville: Abingdon, 1994), with reflections on feminist maternal theology on pp. 104–105. Valerie Saiving's thoughts on women and pride are found in "The Human Situation: A Feminine View," *Journal of Religion* (Apr. 1960).

My understanding of the task of practical theology is partly guided by Don S. Browning's *A Fundamental Practical Theology: Descriptive and Strategic Proposals* (Minneapolis: Fortress, 1996). I borrow the phrase "wisdom of

185

experience" from Rodney J. Hunter's "The Future of Pastoral Theology," *Pastoral Psychology,* 1980, *29*(1), p. 65.

CHAPTER ONE

———

Anne Higonnet's portrayal of new ways of seeing children in *Pictures of Innocence: The History and Crisis of Ideal Childhood* (New York: Thames and Hudson, 1998) proved especially pivotal for my thinking in this chapter. Direct quotes come from pp. 12, 209, and 224. The claim about the discovery of children appears in Philippe Ariès, *Centuries of Childhood: A Social History of the Family,* Robert Baldick, trans. (New York: Vintage Books, 1962). More recent histories that informed my thinking include Steven Mintz and Susan Kellogg, *Domestic Revolutions: A Social History of American Family Life* (New York: Free Press, 1988); John Demos, *Past, Present, and Personal: The Family and the Life Course in American History* (New York: Oxford University Press, 1985), with a quotation from p. 10; Viviana A. Zelizer, *Pricing the Priceless Child: The Changing Social Value of Children* (Princeton: Princeton University Press, 1994); Karin Calvert, *Children in the House: The Material Culture of Early Childhood, 1600–1900* (Boston: Northeastern University Press, 1992), with quotations from pp. 6–7; and N. Ray Hiner and Joseph M. Hawes, eds., *Growing Up in America: Children in Historical Perspective* (Urbana and Chicago: University of Illinois Press, 1985).

To understand major demographic changes, I found useful Ron Lesthaeghe's "A Century of Demographic and

Cultural Change in Western Europe: An Exploration of Underlying Dimensions," *Population and Development Review,* 1983, *9*(3), 411–435; two chapters in Arlene S. Skolnick and Jerome H. Skolnick's edited collection *Family in Transition,* 9th ed. (New York: Addison-Wesley, 1997), the first by Dennis A. Ahlburg and Carol J. De Vita ("New Realities of the American Family," pp. 21–29, with the statistic about the percentage of families including children on p. 24) and the second by Donald Hernandez, with David E. Myers ("Revolutions in Children's Lives," pp. 256–266); and Tom W. Smith's "The Emerging 21st-Century American Family," a report from the National Opinion Research Center, available on the Internet at www.norc.uchicago.edu. The Children's Defense Fund, under the leadership of Marion Wright Edelman, also publishes an annual report, *The State of America's Children* (Boston: Beacon, 2000), with information available on the Defense Fund's website (www.childrensdefense.org).

I found the two contrasting views of our economic responsibility for children in Victor R. Fuchs and Diane M. Reklis, "America's Children: Economic Perspectives and Policy Options," *Science* (Jan. 3, 1992), *255,* 41–46; and Mercy Amba Oduyoye, "A Coming Home to Myself: The Childless Woman in the West African Space," in *Liberating Eschatology: Essays in Honor of Letty M. Russell,* Margaret A. Farley and Serene Jones, eds. (Louisville: Westminster John Knox, 1999), pp. 105–120. The numbers on poverty and the quotation from Daniel Patrick Moynihan appear in "Social Justice in the Next Century," *America,* 1991, *165*(6), 136. I found information about the saying that children should be "seen but not heard" in

H. L. Mencken, *A New Dictionary of Quotations on Historical Principles from Ancient and Modern Sources* (New York: Knopf, 1942), p. 169. Judith Rich Harris's comment on the prominence of nature and nurture is on p. 1 of *The Nurture Assumption: Why Children Turn Out the Way They Do* (New York: Touchstone, 1999).

CHAPTER TWO

I came across Ellen T. Charry's dismissal of psychology in "Who's Minding the Children?" *Theology Today,* 2000, *56*(4), 452–453 (article on pp. 451–455). Anna Freud's advice to Robert Coles is described on p. xv of his Introduction to *The Spiritual Life of Children* (Boston: Houghton Mifflin, 1990). Alice Miller makes the claim about the sweeping influence of her book on p. 2 of *The Drama of the Gifted Child: The Search for the True Self,* completely revised and updated with a new introduction by the author, Ruth Ward, trans. (New York: Basic Books, 1994). I elaborate on the story she tells on pp. 87–89 of a two-year-old boy who wants his parent's ice cream. My discussion of children's love of others draws on her comments on pp. viii-ix of the Foreword to the First Edition, which was published in 1981. Her dismissal of religion that I cite is on p. 11 of this same edition. The concept of "poisonous pedagogy" and the longer quote from Miller at the end of my chapter comes from p. xi of a later book, *For Your Own Good: Hidden*

Cruelty in Child-rearing and the Roots of Violence, Hilde-
garde and Hunter Hannum, trans. (New York: Farrar,
Straus, and Giroux, 1983).

On Christianity's justification of punishment, see
Philip Greven's *Spare the Child: The Religious Roots of
Punishment and the Psychological Impact of Physical Abuse*
(New York: Vintage Books, 1990). He acknowledges
Miller's powerful influence on p. xiii, and his reference to
the Bible's instrumental role is on p. 6. Mary Pipher's
comparison of her contribution to Miller's, her view of
girls' conflicts, and her comments on her own religious
background can be found on pp. 36, 37, and 71 of *Reviv-
ing Ophelia: Saving the Selves of Adolescent Girls* (New
York: Ballantine Books, 1994). The classic study on the
"Catch-22" women face is found in I. K. Broverman, D.
M. Broverman, and F. E. Clarkson, "Sex Role Stereotypes
and Clinical Judgments of Mental Health," *Journal of
Consulting & Clinical Psychology,* 1970, *34,* 1–7. Dan Kindlon and Michael Thompson coin the phrase "culture of
cruelty" and discuss the biblical Cain on p. 19 of *Raising
Cain: Protecting the Emotional Life of Boys* (Ballantine
Books, 1999). Another similar bestseller is William Pol-
lack's *Real Boys: Rescuing Our Sons from the Myths of Boy-
hood* (New York: Owl Books, 1999).

The characterization of Luther and love is found on
p. 131 of William H. Lazareth's *Luther on the Christian
Home: An Application of the Social Ethics of the Reformation*
(Philadelphia: Muhlenberg Press, 1960). For alternative
psychological ways to understand children and parenting,
I relied upon D. W. Winnicott's *The Maturational Processes*

and the Facilitating Environment: Studies in the Theory of Emotional Development (New York: International Universities Press, 1965) and Heinz Kohut's *How Does Analysis Cure?* (Chicago: University of Chicago Press, 1984).

For the development of the idea of "good enough mother," see Winnicott, *The Maturational Processes and the Facilitating Environment: Studies in the Theory of Emotional Development* (New York: International Universities Press, 1965) and Bruno Bettelheim, *A Good Enough Parent: A Book on Child-Rearing* (New York: Vintage Books, 1987).

CHAPTER THREE

This chapter reaps the benefits of a book edited by Marcia Bunge, *The Child in Christian Thought* (Grand Rapids: Eerdmans, 2001). Bunge's own comments on Francke appear in her chapter "The Child in 18th Century German Pietism: Perspectives from the Work of A. H. Francke," pp. 247–278. I found the Christian qualification of children's innocence in Augustine on p. 84 of Martha Ellen Stortz's chapter "'Where or When Was Your Servant Innocent?' Augustine on Childhood" and in Menno Simons on p. 194 of Keith Graber Miller's chapter "Complex Innocence, Obligatory Nurturance, and Parental Vigilance: 'The Child' in the Work of Menno Simons." Miller's comment about the community's essential role appears on this same page. Catherine A. Brekus's characterization of Edwards's "double image" appears on p. 312 of her chapter "Children of Wrath, Children of Grace: Jonathan Edwards and the Puritan Culture of Childrearing," and also in *The Child in Christian Thought*.

Philip Greven claims Christian theology is rooted in punishment on p. 8 of *Spare the Child: The Religious Roots of Punishment and the Psychological Impact of Physical Abuse* (New York: Vintage Books, 1990). The two texts to which I refer that follow Alice Miller and Greven's ideas are Donald Capps, *The Child's Song: The Religious Abuse of Children* (Louisville: Westminster John Knox, 1995) and Stephen Pattison, "'Suffer Little Children': The Challenge of Child Abuse and Neglect to Theology," *Theology and Sexuality*, 1998, *9*, 36–58. The comments by the high school principal and youth minister on use of the terminology of sin come from a study cited on p. 19 of James Davison Hunter's essay "When Psychotherapy Replaces Religion," *Public Interest*, Spring 2000, *139*, 5–21.

For the helpful views on discipline, see Bruno Bettelheim, "Punishment Vs. Discipline," *Atlantic*, 1985, *256*(5), 51–59 (quotations are from pp. 52 and 54); Thomas Gordon, *Parent Effectiveness Training: The Proven Program for Raising Responsible Children* (New York: Three Rivers Press, 2000); and Anne Eggebroten, "Sparing the Rod: Biblical Discipline and Parental Discipline," *The Other Side*, Apr. 1987, pp. 26–32 (her quotation of Gordon's comment on parental power is from p. 29; Gordon's emphasis). The concluding comments on freedom, sin, and liberation appear in Samuel Wells, "Regeneration," *Christian Century*, Mar. 22–29, 2000, p. 335.

Chapter Four

In formulating this chapter, I found particularly helpful Todd David Whitmore's "Children: An Undeveloped Theme in Catholic Teaching," in *The Challenge of Global Stewardship: Roman Catholic Responses,* Maura A. Ryan and Todd David Whitmore, eds. (Notre Dame, Ind.: University of Notre Dame, 1997). Quotations are from pp. 175 and 179. Conversations with my Vanderbilt colleague Douglas Meeks also made a decided difference. Some of the ideas we discussed can be found in his chapter "Trinity, Community, and Power," in *Trinity, Community, and Power,* M. Douglas Meeks, ed. (Nashville: Abingdon/Kingswood, 2000).

This chapter also benefits from Bunge's *The Child in Christian Thought.* To understand children in the New Testament, I turned to Judith Gundry-Volf's chapter "The Least and the Greatest: Children in the New Testament," pp. 29–60. Her assertion about the exemplary regard of Christianity for children appears on p. 39, her interpretation of Jesus imitating women is on p. 43, and her claims about the radicality of his actions are on pp. 58 and 60. The quotation about children's status in antiquity is found on p. 58 of another Gundry-Volf essay, "Between Text and Sermon: Mark 9:33–37," *Interpretation,* 1999, 53(1), 57–61. On "gift" terminology in Calvin and Schleiermacher respectively, I was helped by two other chapters in Bunge: Barbara Pitkin's "'The Heritage of the Lord': Children in the Theology of John Calvin," pp.

160–193 (and personal correspondence with Pitkin) and Dawn DeVries's "'Be Converted and Become as Little Children': Friedrich Schleiermacher on the Religious Significance of Childhood," pp. 329–349. DeVries's remark about Schleiermacher's contemporary relevance is from p. 349. Schleiermacher talks about gifts and children on pp. 35–36 and about Christ as the greatest gift on p. 45 of *Christmas Eve: Dialogues on the Incarnation,* Terrence N. Tice, trans. (Richmond, Va.: John Knox, 1967). Calvin's praise of children is plentiful, but my specific references come from *Calvin's Commentaries,* 46 vols. (Edinburgh: Calvin Translation Society, 1843–1855), Commentary on the Psalms 1:96 and 5:110–111 and Commentary on Genesis 1:537.

My reading of the scriptural blessing of children as a social and political statement relies significantly upon James L. Bailey, "Experiencing the Kingdom as a Little Child: A Rereading of Mark 10:13–16," *Word-&-World,* Winter 1995, *15,* 58–67. His claim about the twofold nature of gift and task is on p. 62. He in turn relies heavily on Ched Myers, *Binding the Strong Man: A Political Reading of Mark's Story of Jesus* (Maryknoll, N.Y.: Orbis, 1988), pp. 266–271. Bailey also pointed me to two texts on Jesus' physical actions: Vernon K. Robbins, "Pronouncement Stories and Jesus' Blessing of the Children: A Rhetorical Approach," *Semeia,* 1983, *29,* 62–70; and John Dominic Crossan, *Jesus: A Revolutionary Biography* (San Francisco: HarperSanFrancisco, 1994), p. 64. I also used James Francis, "Children and Childhood in the New Testament," in *The Family in Theological Perspective,* Stephen C. Barton, ed. (Edinburgh, Scotland: T & T Clark, 1996), pp. 65–85; and David G.

Hunter, "Children," *Encyclopedia of Early Christianity*, 2nd ed. (New York: Garland, 1997), pp. 237–238. The quotation of Martin Luther on Matt. 25 is from *Luther's Works*, Jaroslav Pelikan and Helmut Lehmann, eds., 55 vols. (St. Louis: Concordia, 1955–1986), vol. 44, p. 85.

I found few articles on the "household codes" and children. To rethink the codes, I depended upon Lewis R. Donelson, *Colossians, Ephesians, First and Second Timothy, and Titus* (Louisville: Westminster John Knox, 1996); David L. Balch, *Let Wives Be Submissive: The Domestic Code in 1 Peter* (Atlanta: Scholars, 1981); and James D. G. Dunn, "The Household Rules in the New Testament," in Barton (ed.), *The Family in Theological Perspective,* pp. 43–63. Quotations on Colossians and Ephesians are from pp. 50 and 102 of Donelson's commentary.

CHAPTER FIVE

———

This chapter draws on previous work I have done on feminism and family, especially *Also a Mother* and "Let the Child Come Revisited: Feminist Theologians on Children," in Bunge's *The Child in Christian Thought*, pp. 446–473.

To characterize secular feminist views, I quote Jessie Bernard's bold statement from p. 48 of *The Future of Motherhood* (New York: Dial Press, 1974); Maura A. Ryan's characterization of reproductive debates from her entry on "Abortion" on p. 2 of the *Dictionary of Feminist Theologies,* Letty Russell and J. Shannon Clarkson, eds.

(Louisville: Westminster/John Knox, 1996); bell hooks's praise of feminism on p. 72 of *Feminism Is for Everybody: Passionate Politics* (Cambridge, Mass.: South End Press, 2000); and Judith Stacey's worries about profamily developments in "Are Feminists Afraid to Leave Home? The Challenge of Conservative Pro-Family Feminism," in *What Is Feminism? A Reexamination,* Juliet Mitchell and Ann Oakley, eds. (New York: Pantheon, 1986), pp. 208–237. I found the derisive mention of the bumper sticker on p. 55 of Barbara Dafoe Whitehead's notorious essay "Dan Quayle Was Right," *Atlantic Monthly* (Apr. 1993), pp. 47–84.

To understand how feminists have redefined children as work, I turn to Hilda Scott, *Working Your Way to the Bottom: The Feminization of Poverty* (London: Pandora, 1984), with quotations from pp. x, xi, and 163; Rhona Mahony, *Kidding Ourselves: Breadwinning, Babies, and Bargaining Power* (New York: Basic, 1995); and Arlie Hochschild with Anne Machung, *The Second Shift: Working Parents and the Revolution of Home* (New York: Viking Penguin, 1989), with the time use studies appearing on pp. 3–4.

Some of my thoughts on mutuality and children spring from Carter Heyward's *When Boundaries Betray Us: Beyond Illusions of What Is Ethical in Therapy and Life* (New York: HarperCollins, 1993), with a quotation from p. 10 (her emphasis). For more substantive help in reimagining children as the labor of love, see Christine Gudorf's "Parenting, Mutual Love and Sacrifice," in *Women's Consciousness, Women's Conscience: A Reader in Feminist Ethics,* Barbara Hilkert Andolsen, Christine E.

Gudorf, and Mary D. Pelauer, eds. (San Francisco: HarperSanFrancisco, 1985). Quotations come from pp. 176, 181, 182, 186, 189, and 190.

In considering the role of sacrifice and love's limits, I refer to Brita L. Gill-Austern, "Love Understood as Self-Sacrifice and Self-Denial: What Does It Do to Women?" *Through the Eyes of Women: Insights for Pastoral Care,* Jeanne Stevenson Moessner, ed. (Philadelphia: Westminster John Knox, 1996), pp. 304–321, with quotations from pp. 315 and 318; Don S. Browning, Bonnie J. Miller-McLemore, Pamela D. Couture, K. Brynoff Lyon, and Robert M. Franklin, *From Culture Wars to Common Ground: Religion and the American Family Debate* (Louisville: Westminster/John Knox, 1997), with quotations from pp. 153–154 and 293; Barbara Hilkert Andolsen, "Agape in Feminist Ethics," *Journal of Religious Ethics,* 1981, *9*(1), 69–83; and finally, Herbert Anderson, "Between Rhetoric and Reality: Women and Men as Equal Partners in Home, Church and the Marketplace," *Word and World: Theology for Christian Ministry,* 1997, *17*(4), 385.

CHAPTER SIX

Pam Couture, friend, colleague, and strong advocate for children, helped me name this final vision of children as agents. I refer to her book *Seeing Children, Seeing God: A Practical Theology of Children and Poverty* (Nashville: Abingdon, 2000), with quotations from pp. 13 and 47. Long before I began this research, another good friend,

Paula Cooey, sent me her essay "That Every Child Who Wants Might Learn to Dance," *Cross Currents: The Journal of the Association for Religion and Intellectual Life,* 1998, *48*(2), 185–197. Her more theoretical statement of the claim in her essay title appears on p. 101 of her book *Family, Freedom, and Faith: Building Community* (Louisville: Westminster/John Knox, 1996) where she also talks about children as persons on p. 103.

For an exploration of children's bodyrights, see Christine Gudorf's *Body, Sex, and Pleasure: Reconstructing Christian Sexual Ethics* (Cleveland: Pilgrim, 1994). My quotations come from pp. 161 and 203. Her depiction of her children's influence appears on p. 177 of "Parenting, Mutual Love, and Sacrifice," in *Women's Consciousness and Women's Conscience.* Her most explicit statement about children's rights is "Children, Rights of," in *The New Dictionary of Catholic Social Thought,* Judith A Dwyer, ed. (Collegeville, Minn.: Liturgical Press, 1994), pp. 143–147. For her ideas on parental growth, see "Sacrificial and Parental Spiritualities," in *Religion, Feminism, and the Family,* Anne Carr and Mary Stewart Van Leeuwen, eds. (Louisville: Westminster John Knox, 1996), pp. 295–298; and "Dissecting Parenthood: Infertility, in Vitro, and Other Lessons in Why and How We Parent," *Conscience,* 1994, *15*(3), 22.

The commentary on the sexual abuse scandal in the Catholic church comes from Christopher Beem, "Of Troubled Hearts," *Sightings,* May 30, 2002, Martin Marty Center (http://divinity.uchicago.edu/martinmartyinterim.html). The statistics on child poverty are from the Children's Defense Fund's *The State of America's Children,*

Yearbook 2002, Marion Wright Edelman, ed. (Boston: Beacon, 2002).

In considering children as spiritual agents, I turn to my own previous writings, Chapter Seven of *Also a Mother*, quoting pp. 146 and 155; and "Contemplation in the Midst of Chaos," in *The Scope of Our Art: The Vocation of Theological Teachers,* Gregory Jones and Stephanie Paulsell, eds. (Grand Rapids: Eerdmans, 2001), pp. 48–74. Of further help were Margaret Hebblethwaite's *Motherhood and God* (London: Geoffrey Chapman, 1984), with the quotations from p. 1; Kathryn Allen Rabuzzi, *Mother with Child: Transformations Through Childbirth* (Bloomington: Indiana University Press, 1994), with the quotation from p. xv; Tikva Frymer-Kensky, "Birth Silence and *Motherprayer,*" *Criterion,* Spring/Summer 1995, p. 28, and her book of prayers, *Motherprayer: The Pregnant Woman's Spiritual Companion* (New York: Riverhead Books, 1995); Wendy M. Wright, "Living the Already But Not Yet: The Spiritual life of the American Catholic Family," *Warren Lecture Series in Catholic Studies,* no. 25, University of Tulsa, Mar. 21, 1993, with quotations from pp. 2–3; and Elizabeth Ann Dreyer, "Asceticism Reconsidered," *Weavings: A Journal of the Christian Spiritual Life,* 1988, *3*(6), p. 14 (article on pp. 6–15).

Clarissa W. Atkinson quotes Jerome on p. 239 of *The Oldest Vocation: Christian Motherhood in the Middle Ages* (Ithaca and London: Cornell University Press, 1991). The philosopher who seems surprised to discover children as philosophers is Gareth B. Matthews; I cite his words from p. 5 of *The Philosophy of Childhood* (Cambridge,

Mass.: Harvard University Press, 1994). Kathleen Norris complains about adult misperceptions on pp. 59–60 of *Cloister Walk* (New York: Riverhead Books, 1996). Daniel N. Stern admits his ignorance about the mother's development on p. 5 of *The Birth of the Mother: How the Motherhood Experience Changes You Forever* (New York: Basic Books, 1998). The suggestion for taking a "second breath" comes from Robert C. Morris, "The Second Breath: Frustration as a Doorway to Daily Spiritual Practice," *Weavings: A Journal of the Christian Spiritual Life,* 1998, *13*(2), 37–45.

Finally, I found Beverly Harrison's words on the feminist agenda especially helpful from p. 15 of "Situating the Dilemma of Abortion Historically," *Conscience: A Newsjournal of Prochoice Catholic Opinion,* 1990, *11*(2), and p. 31 of *Our Right to Choose: Toward a New Ethic of Abortion* (Boston: Beacon, 1983).

EPILOGUE

———

I thank Pinita Gurdian Vijil, who spoke so powerfully in August 2001, and her "Prayer for My Children," *La Prensa,* July 21, 1977, Elena Olazagasti-Segovia, trans. The other Nicaraguan woman whom I cite is not someone I met but rather someone quoted in Mary Guerrera Congo's "The Truth Will Set You Free, But First It Will Make You Crazy," in *Sacred Dimensions of Women's Experience,* Elizabeth Dodson Gray, ed. (Wellesley, Mass.: Roundtable, 1988), p. 83. Gregory Jones raises the question about "happiness" as a parental desire for children in the essay "Our Children's Happiness," *Christian Century* (May 19–26, 1999), p. 595.

Black feminist Patricia Hill Collins suggests the term "othermothering" on pp. 119–120 of *Black Feminist Thought: Knowledge, Consciousness, and the Politics of Empowerment* (New York: Routledge, 1991). For two good womanist developments of this idea, see Delores S. Williams, *Sisters in the Wilderness: The Challenge of Womanist God-Talk* (Maryknoll, New York: Orbis, 1993), pp. 34–59; and Teresa E. Snorton, "The Legacy of the African-American Matriarch: New Perspectives for Pastoral Care," in *Through the Eyes of Women: Insights for Pastoral Care* (Minneapolis: Augsburg Fortress, 1996), pp. 50–65. Mercy Amba Oduyoye names parenting a "religious duty" on pp. 23–24 of "Poverty and Motherhood," *Concilium,* 1989, *206,* 23–30.

On parenting as a social practice, see Beverly Wildung Harrison with Shirley Cloyes, "Theology and Morality of Procreative Choice," in *Making the Connections: Essays in Feminist Social Ethics,* Carol S. Robb, ed. (Boston: Beacon, 1985), p. 130; and Lisa Sowle Cahill, *Sex, Gender, and Christian Ethics* (Cambridge: Cambridge University Press, 1996), pp. 48, 201 (her emphasis), and 207. Cahill's comments about her own experience are from pp. xii-xiii of *Family: A Christian Social Perspective* (Minneapolis: Fortress, 2000).

As I neared completion of this book, I benefited from hearing Jeanne Stevenson Moessner speak on adoption, now published in *Spirit of Adoption: At Home in God's*

Family (Minneapolis: Augsburg Fortress, 2003). Paula Cooey discusses reinvigorating godparenting on p. 102 of *Family, Freedom, and Faith: Building Community* (Louisville: Westminster/John Knox, 1996). Harrison's claim about the power of nurture is found on pp. 47–48 of "The Power of Anger in the Work of Love: Christian Ethics for Women and Other Strangers," *Union Seminary Quarterly Review*, 1981, *36*, 41–57.

ACKNOWLEDGMENTS

———

A book that percolates over several years accumulates debt in a lot of places. Without a few turning-point pep talks from good friends—Martha Stortz, Pamela Couture, Stephanie Meis, Renita Weems, Paula Cooey, Brita Gill-Austern, Dorothy Bass, Mark Miller-McLemore, Herbert Anderson, and Don Browning—this book might not have seen the light of day. These friends may not remember the exact times they listened, encouraged, coaxed, and cajoled. But their commonsense counsel as well as their unadulterated comments of appreciation for my work got me through many otherwise disappointing writing days and a midlife crisis or two.

Some of these same people, and many others, responded to questions I asked of their expertise or read initial proposals, chapters, portions of chapters, the entire manuscript, or articles related to this book: Martha Stortz, Pamela Couture, Dorothy Bass, Volney Gay, Sallie McFague, Don Browning, Kathleen Greider, Ulrike Guthrie, Leonard Hummel, Marcia Bunge, Cristina Traina, Catherine Brekus, Marcia Riggs, Sheila Briggs, Barbara Pitkin, Margaret Bendroth, Judith Gundry-Volf, Stephanie Paulsell, Clark Gilpin, Douglas Meeks, Herbert Anderson, Chris Schlauch, and Brad Wigger. Valuable feedback from each person corrected oversights, pointed me toward new ideas, and in some cases changed the course of the book.

The editorial staff at Jossey-Bass also deserves praise. The late Sarah Polster, Sheryl Fullerton, and, most decisively and with welcomed cheerfulness, Julianna Gustafson guided the book through a desirable, even if sometimes arduous, metamorphosis. I am also indebted to the painstakingly detailed advice of three outside manuscript reviewers and the additional counsel, cheerleading, and clarifying chapter reworkings of development editor Naomi Wolf.

For the actual material conditions of research, I am grateful to Henry Luce III, chair and CEO; John Cook, president; and Michael Gilligan, program director for theology, of the Henry Luce Foundation, which afforded the wonderful gift of a second semester of sabbatical as a Henry Luce III Fellow in Theology in 1999–2000; and to Daniel Aleshire, executive director of the Association of Theological Schools, and both Matthew Zyniewicz and Christopher Wilkins, coordinators of Faculty Grant Programs, who facilitate the program and Fellows' conference. I thank Vanderbilt University, the Divinity School, my faculty colleagues, and dean James Hudnut-Beumler for the day job that is the excuse for producing books in the first place, as well as Nancy Weatherwax, Katharine Baker, and Eileen Campbell-Reed for their university- and Luce-supported research assistance. I am especially appreciative of Campbell-Reed's helpful work on the Questions for Reflection and her reading of the manuscript. I also appreciate Brad Wigger and Diana Garland's invitation to join other authors I admired in the Families and Faith Book Series, sponsored by the Division of Religion of the Lilly Endowment, Inc.

Several groups responded to research presentations with constructive suggestions: the 2000–01 Luce conference participants; members of the Child in Theology Project, directed by Marcia Bunge and supported by the Lilly Endowment, Inc.; members of the Study Group on Theological Dimensions of Family at the Society for Pastoral Theology; students and faculty at Louisville Theological Seminary; and participants at the Society for Pastoral Theology, the Association of Practical Theology, the Society of Christian Ethics, and the American Academy of Religion, where I delivered academic papers based on selected chapters. Finally, I especially valued the forthright observations of those caught up most immediately in thinking about children: all those who shared inner qualms on soccer sidelines, at coffee hours, during teacher-parent conferences, and in myriad other places; ministry and doctoral students in courses; and volunteers

Acknowledgments

in local focus groups and classes at Clark Memorial United Methodist Church, Vine Street Christian Church, Woodmont Christian Church, Brookmeade Congregational Church, St. Ann's Episcopal Church, and Brentwood United Methodist Church.

This book sorely tested an earlier claim of mine that women can have children and write books. Sometimes the very intensity of my family life forced me to dig down deep to resources I didn't know I had. Mark and my three sons, Chris, Matt, and Daniel, helped simply by carrying on life as usual around me. I'm grateful for the joy and steadfast love my family brings on a fairly regular basis. They remind me of the serious relativity of my work in the wider scheme of life.

B.J.M.-M.

THE AUTHOR

———

B onnie J. Miller-McLemore is professor of pastoral theology and counseling at Vanderbilt University Divinity School and the mother of three boys. Recipient of a prestigious Henry Luce III Fellow in Theology grant, she is widely recognized for her writing on the dilemmas of work, families, women, and children; among her several books and articles are the books *From Culture Wars to Common Ground: Religion and the American Family Debate* (coauthored with Browning, Couture, Lyon, and Franklin) and *Also a Mother: Work and Family as Theological Dilemma.* Ordained in the Christian Church (Disciples of Christ), she has also served as associate minister, chaplain, and pastoral counselor.

INDEX

Friedan, B., 113

From Culture Wars to Common Ground (Miller-McLemore and others), 131, 134–135

Frustration, moments of, capitalizing on, 154, 155

Frymer-Kensky, T., 156

Fundamentalist Christian groups, 116–117

G

Gender bias in therapy, 35

Gender roles, 107, 109, 110, 111

Genesis, 103

Genesis 4:7, 51

Gift: idea of, from scripture, 94–96, 97–101; market-driven eclipse of, 88–94; overview of, 83–84; the Pastoral Letters eclipsing, 84–88; reclaiming, 101–104

Gift exchange, 92–93, 102

Gifted children, 32

Gill-Austern, B., 131–132

Gilligan, C., 34

Girl-poisoning culture, 25, 33–35, 36; blaming, consequences of, 52

Girls: cultural view of, changing, need for, 36, 44, 45, 48; and uneven distribution of child rearing, 122–123; value of, in Greco-Roman society, 97

Giving gifts, sharing in, 92–93, 102

God: created in image of, 138, 140; differing views of, 78; entrusting children to, 157; grace of, 71, 78; kingdom of, 95, 96, 99, 100, 101, 104, 127–128, 169; love of, 170; reflection on motherhood and, 152

Godparenting, 166, 167

Golden Rule, 29

Gonzalez, E., 91

Good life, 169–170

Good-enough parent, 49

Gordon, T., 79–80

Grace: appreciation for, 54; of God, 71, 78; means of, 149; and mutuality, 134; need for, 52; sin and, relationship between, 59–60, 66, 68, 74–75, 81; toward children, case for, 59

Great Judgment, 100, 101

Greco-Roman society, 85, 87, 96–97, 99

Greed, 63, 73

Greven, P., 37, 38, 46, 57, 58, 59, 76

Growth: child's inner, seedbed of, 49; spiritual, from parenting, 155–157

Gudorf, C., 126, 127, 131, 132, 141, 142, 143, 144, 145, 149–150, 156–157

Guilt, 60, 61, 68, 73

Guilt trip, relief from, desire for, 18

Gundry-Volf, J., 96–97, 99, 100, 101, 102

H

Hannah, 98

Harris, J., 17, 18

Harrison, B., 119, 159, 160, 168

Head-of-household, male. *See* Patriarchy

Heart, loss of, imperative to avoid, 86, 87

Hebblethwaite, M., 151–152

Hebrews 11:1, 160

Hebrews 12:5–11, 57

Hebrews 12:6, 37

Hellenistic texts, 100

Heyward, C., 129, 130

Hierarchy, 129, 130, 131, 142. *See also* Patriarchy

High school parties, 143

Higonnet, A., 19–20

Hochschild, A., 121

Honest communication, 79

hooks, b., 110
Hospitality, practicing, 100–101
Household codes (scriptural), 84–88;
    comments on, 93–94
Household demographics, 11–12
Human decency, adolescent defiance
    of, 72, 73
Human frailty, 52, 53, 54, 67–68, 71
Human relations, restructuring,
    need for, 108. *See also* Family
    relationships
Humbleness, 96
Huron Indians, 69
Hurried child, 10–11, 18
Hutterites, 72
Hypervigilance, 89

I

Idealization, 41, 43, 49, 93, 107; chal-
    lenging, 120, 125, 128
Imperfect world, 74–81
Incentive, fear as, 75
Incest, 109. *See also* Sexual abuse
Income factor, 11–12
Independence, 67
Indifference toward other children,
    12
Individual good and common good,
    169–170
Industrial Revolution, the, 3, 4
Infanticide, 97, 99
Infantilization, 143
Infants: accountability of, 73; bap-
    tism of, 70, 71, 76; as gift, 103;
    greed of, 63, 73; needs of, 39;
    sinfulness of, rigidity about, 70
Innocence, 14, 19–20, 21, 22, 66, 151;
    lingering notion of, 143; myth
    of, debunking, 52; and sin,
    qualifying and differentiating,
    68–73
Insight, gaining, from children,
    151–152
Interdependence, 67

International public, role of, 140
Interpretation of Dreams (Freud), 28
Irresponsibility, sphere of, protected,
    131
Isaac, 46, 98, 103, 104
Israel, 98, 104
Italian prayer books, 156

J

Jerome, 149
Jesuit missionaries, 69
Jesus: on children, 58, 85, 86, 94–96,
    97–101, 102, 170; conception of,
    98; crucifixion of, 37, 38, 57;
    and ethic of love, 127–128; as
    gift, 92, 98–99; on power, 80;
    relationship between the disci-
    ples and, 77; sacrifices of, 127;
    on women's work, 100
Jewish prayer tradition, 156
Jewish society, 85, 98, 99, 116
Joy-filled engagement, encouraging,
    147
Junk culture, 34
Justice in marriage, 134
Justice, social. *See* Social justice
Justification, 37–38, 46, 166

K

Kellogg, S., 1
Kindlon, D., 25, 50–51
Kingdom of God: receiving, 95, 96,
    99, 100, 101, 104, 169; rich re-
    turn in, 127–128
Knowing children, 18, 19–23, 79,
    133, 151–152, 157
Kohut, H., 40–41, 42, 43, 48–49, 89

L

Labor of love, 124–135
Lamott, A., xvii, xviii, xix, 1
Learning from children, 39
Less-privileged children, 4, 8, 9, 12,
    19, 89–90, 91, 97

Moral agency, robbing children of, 14, 20, 52

Moral agents, 138, 139–148

Moral and religious development: challenges of, preparation for, struggle to, 27; community responsibility for, 72, 75, 76; describing, schemas for, 71; and gaining control, 52; intricacies of, 66; nuances of, 54; parental influence on, 75–76; trajectory of, 80–81

Mother role, change in, 9

Motherhood: idealization of, 107; and meaning, 152; overwhelming nature of, 111–112; personhood independent from, 107; reconsideration of, 112, 113, 114, 115; sacred dimension and realities of, 150; as transformative, 155–156

Motherhood feminists, 113, 114, 119, 120, 138

Motivation, fear as, 75

Moynihan, D. P., 12–13

Mutual love, 126, 127, 128–135

Mutuality: expectations of, providing, 132–133; in family relationships, 114, 118; in therapy, 129

N

Narcissism in children, 41, 42, 43, 49

Narcissistically needy parents, 89; blaming, consequences of, 52; children as victims of, 30–33; needs of, curbing, 54

Nature versus nurture debate, 17–18, 51

Negotiation, 79

Nicaragua, 161–162

Nonentities, children as, 91, 92, 102

Noninnocence, 69, 71

Norris, K., 151

Nuclear family. *See* Traditional family

Nurture: emotional, importance of, 15; learning to, consequence of, 169; nature versus, debate over, 17–18, 51

Nurture Assumption, The (Harris), 17

O

Obedience, 60, 85, 87, 88, 104; assumption of, inverting, 97–98; differing views of, 78; unquestioning, 37, 76

Obsession of parents, 89–90

Of Women Born (Rich), 113

Operating Instructions: A Journal of My Sons's First Year (Lamott), xvii

Original sin, 13, 51, 59, 63, 65

"Othermothering," 165

Overidentification, 157

Overprogramming, 10

Oversight, 71, 167

Ownership, 79, 87, 141

P

Palestinian society, early, 98

Paradox of power, 79–80

Parental Effectiveness Training (PET), 79–80

Parenting: ambiguities of, 51; challenges of, addressing, shying away from, 61; essence of, 75–76; failure in, 48–49, 53, 67–68; spiritual growth from, 155–157; spirituality of, 152, 153; tasks added to, 7–8

Pastoral Letters, 84–88

Patriarchal family. *See* Traditional family

Patriarchy, 85, 86, 87–88, 97, 98, 107, 114, 116; and children's rights, 146; status quo of, desire for preserving, 117. *See also* Hierarchy

217

Religion, role of, discounting, 47
Religious development. *See* Moral and religious development
Religious discipline, 15, 16–17, 53, 76, 163–164, 167
Religious doctrine, distortion of, 46–47
Religious tradition, preserving, contending with, 116–117
Repressed feelings, dealing with, 47
Reprimand, effect of, 86–87
Reproduction of Mothering, The (Chodorow), 113
Reproductive rights, 107, 108–109. *See also* Abortion
Respecting children: aspects of, 38–45; comprehensive, 147; inherent merit of, 140, 158; lack of, effect of, 31–32; moving beyond, 54, 55; and mutuality, 135; need for, 60–61; through age-appropriate considerations, 79, 143, 145–146; and understanding sin, 65. *See also* Children's rights
Return gifting, 102–103
Reviving Ophelia (Pipher), 25, 33
Rich, A., 113
Robbins, V., 100
Roe v. *Wade,* 106
Romantic child, 20. *See also* Innocence
Rousseau, J., 14
Ruddick, S., 113
Ruether, R. R., 119
Ryan, M., 109

S

Sacrifice, transitional, 131–132
Sacrifices of Jesus, 127
Sacrificial love, 125–128, 132
Saiving, V., 125
Salvation, suffering essential to, 38
Samuel, 98

1 Samuel 2:1–10, 98
Sanctification, 166
Sarah, 98
Schleiermacher, F., 92, 93–94
Schools: issues with, 11; and parties, 143; shootings at, 21
Scott, H., 121, 122
"Seen but not heard" proverb, 10
Self, loss of, 31–32, 34
Self-affirmation, 89
Self-control, 79
Self-determination, deserving of, 144–145
Self-development, 41
Self-diminishment, concern for, 125
Self-disdain, 64
Self-identity, 29, 39
Self-indulgence, greater latitude in, allowing, 131
Self-interest and labor of love, 127, 128
Self-love, debate over, 42–43
Self-sacrificing love, issue of, 125–128, 132
Self-worth, 40, 41
Sex, paying children for, 91
Sexual abuse, 33, 109, 141–142. *See also* Child abuse
Sexuality, 27
Shame, 60, 61, 68
Shaping children, 46–55
Silence and solitude, 149, 154
Simons, M., 69, 70–71, 72, 74, 75, 76
Sin: of adultism, 158; appreciation for, 54; awareness of, awakening to, 61–62; condemnation of, 62; and evil, psychological view of, 50, 51, 52–53, 54; and grace, relationship between, 59–60, 66, 68, 74–75, 81; and innocence, qualifying and differentiating, 68–73; language of, changing, 62–63; and love, 125; and mutuality, 134; original, 13,

Vulnerability, 158

W

Wade, Roe v., 106
War between the sexes, perpetuation of, 123
Wars, using children to fight in, 91
Wells, S., 80, 81
Western European view, 12
Westminster Confession of Faith, 166
When Boundaries Betray Us (Hey-ward), 129
Whining, 31
Whitmore, T. D., 102
Winnicott, D. W., 39, 40, 48, 49
Wisdom, greater, possibility of, 74, 131
Wollstonecraft, M., 107
Woman-centered feminism, 113, 119, 120

Women: roles of, historically, 107; subordination of, 85, 107, 114
Women's rights, 106–107, 109, 111, 112–113. *See also* Feminist movement; Feminist theology
Women's welfare and children's welfare, addressing, issue of, 159–160
Women's work, 100, 101, 108
Wonderment, 150, 151
Work, children as, 120–124, 137; re-thinking ideas of, 125. *See also* Labor of love; Women's work
Workers, using children as, 91
Working mothers, 121, 128
Working-class children, 4, 8
World War II, period after, 15
Worthlessness, sense of, 32
Wright, W., 152

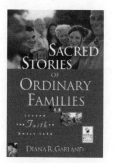

Sacred Stories of Ordinary Families:
Living the Faith in Daily Life

Diana R. Garland

$19.95 Hardcover

ISBN: 0–7879–6257–0

Beautifully written and lyrically told, Diana R. Garland's *Sacred Stories of Ordinary Families* identifies resilience, strength, and faith in the stories of all kinds of families, motivating parents to think about how faith shapes their own family lives.

Drawn from Garland's extensive interviews with 110 families, these stories give voice to families—not just "traditional" first-marriage and biological-children families, but also single-parent families, remarried and blended families, single adults, and older married and widowed adults. Connecting these stories with the Christian story and with biblical texts, Garland explores the diversity of structures these families represent and the ways they seek to live their faith in everyday life.

The rich diversity of families in *Sacred Stories of Ordinary Families* allows the book to resonate with readers of all backgrounds. Readers will be encouraged to connect their own experiences with the sacred and to tell their own stories of faith—to one another and to the congregational community. Grounding their understanding in biblical stories and themes and finding a resource for their own faith in coping with everyday stress and major crises, readers will come away from the book with a stronger sense of how they, too, are living the faith.

Diana R. Garland is the chair of the Social Work Department at Baylor University and director of Baylor's Gheens Center for Christian Family Ministry. A published author, she is also editor of the journal *Family Ministry*. She resides in Waco, Texas, with her husband, David.

[Price subject to change]

Seasons of a Family's Life:
Cultivating the Contemplative Spirit at Home

Wendy M. Wright

$19.95 Hardcover

ISBN: 0–7879–5579–5

Wendy Wright has written a revelatory book about family life. So often taken for granted, so often discounted as drudgery, in her gentle but skilled hands the life of the family is transformed into spiritual reality. As she probes the dish-washing, car-pooling, diaper-changing, curfew-setting reality of everyday life she guides us to sacred ground.
—James P. Wind, president, the Alban Institute

In *Seasons of a Family's Life,* highly respected writer Wendy M. Wright offers a reflective, story-filled examination of the spiritual fabric of domestic life. It focuses on the cultivation of spiritual awareness amidst the ordinary drama of family life and challenges families to wrestle with the great religious questions which have always been part of our human quest: Who in fact *am* I? What is a life well led? What is most essential? What is my responsibility to others? How do I deal with evil? What constitutes the good?

Wright has a particular gift for combining a deep seriousness of purpose, a poetic use of language, and a great sense of humor. With this approach, she explores family life as a context for nurturing spiritual practices, providing parents with suggestions for developing contemplative practices in the home. Each chapter is a lesson in being attentive to the wonder of our experience in family, glimpsing the sacred amidst the chaos of our daily lives.

WENDY M. WRIGHT is a popular speaker at retreats, workshops, and conferences, and a professor of theology at Creighton University. Wright is a frequent contributor to *Weavings* and *Family Ministry,* and is the author of eleven other books. She and her husband live in Omaha, Nebraska, and are the parents of three young adults.

[Price subject to change]